Grill & Barbecue
Cooking

ideals

Ideals Publications Incorporated
Nashville, Tennessee

W9-CBU-785

Contents

A very special thank you to the following for their cooperation and help in supplying selected recipes from their test kitchens and files:

American Dairy Association; American Meat Industry/National Livestock & Meat Board; American Spice Trade Association; 1980 Beef Industry Council; California Olive Industry; Florida Department of Natural Resources/Bureau of Marketing & Extension Services; Kohl's Food Stores; National Pork Producers Council; Ocean Spray; Reynolds Aluminum; Weber-Stephen Products Co.

Copyright © MCMLXXXIV by Ideals Publications Incorporated
All right reserved.
Printed and bound in the United States of America.,

Published by Ideals Publications Incorporated
Nashville, Tennessee 37211

Photo opposite:
Summer Fruit Basket, page 41
Grilled Steaks
Baked Potatoes
Lemonade

Cover recipe:
Orange and Beer Chicken, page 22

Barbecue Basics

Basic Types of Barbecues

There is a wide variety of barbecue grills, from the tabletop hibachi to crowd-size pit barbecues. Generally speaking, the principle of barbecue cooking, no matter what the size of the equipment, is application of even heat to the food to be cooked. The most commonly used barbecues are the round covered kettle, the rectangular firebox with a hinged lid, and the open brazier. For year-round use, gas and electric grills and charcoal cooking kettles are excellent.

Tools and Accessories

A wide range of gadgets and gizmos is readily available for making outdoor grilling easier, but only a few tools are really needed. You'll need long, sturdy tongs for moving hot coals and turning food, a long-handled fork and spatula, and insulated gloves and potholders. For brushing on sauces and marinades, use a nylon brush with a long handle. And, for greater accuracy when timing doneness, a meat thermometer is ideal.

When cooking large cuts of meat that require long cooking or meat with a large amount of fat, an aluminum drip pan is needed. This will catch the fat that would otherwise drip onto the coals and cause flare-ups. Drip pans can be purchased or you can make your own by following the easy instructions below:

How to Make a Drip Pan

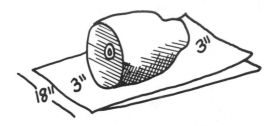

1. Tear off an 18-inch-wide piece of heavy-duty aluminum foil that is at least 3 inches longer than the food to be grilled. Fold to make a double thickness.

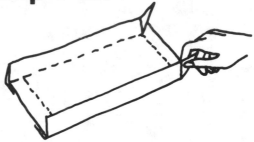

4. Fold edges up and pinch corners.

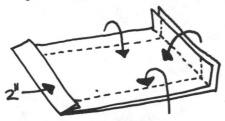

2. Fold all sides in about 2 inches. Press to flatten foil.

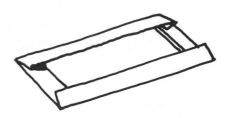

5. Fold corners flat against sides.

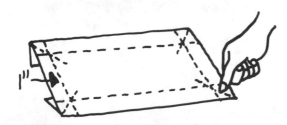

3. Turn foil over. Using your fingernail, score foil about 1 inch from edge. At corners, score diagonally to edge.

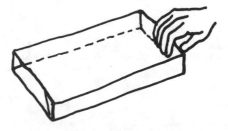

6. Bring all sides up to form pan. Place pan in center of firebox.

Spit Roasting Equipment

Most large grills are made so that spit roasting equipment can be added. Simply stated, this equipment consists of a support, motor, and a pair of forks that slide onto the spit rod at each end to hold the food in place. Before you buy any equipment, be certain that it will fit your barbecue model and that it is well built with a heavy-duty motor.

Cooking Methods

There are four cooking methods that cover the entire range of barbecue cooking. Choose whichever method is appropriate for the type of food you plan to cook.

Grill Cooking — Open Grill

Braziers, hibachies, and built-in brick barbecues are designed for open-grill cooking. Although most manufacturers of covered grills recommend cooking with the lid on, these grills can be used for open-grill cooking too.

Good candidates for open-grill cooking are hamburgers, hot dogs, and steaks. If the food to be cooked is thicker than two inches, cover it loosely with an aluminum foil tent to capture some of the heat. If possible, the grill should be about 6 inches above the heat source.

Cooking — Covered Grill

Most larger barbecue equipment is equipped with a lid which makes it possible to cook even on cold or windy days. The primary function of the cover is to make an oven to trap heat for even cooking. Air flow can be adjusted by opening or closing dampers located on the lid or under the firebox.

Covered grill cooking is especially suited to large food such as roasts or whole poultry. Cooking by this method reduces or eliminates a large amount of the flare-up problem that is often experienced in open-grill cooking, since the air flow is easily adjusted.

Spit Roasting

Nothing beats the succulent juiciness of spit-roasted roasts or poultry. Spit roasting attachments for braziers operate by adjusting the spit up or down in the slots in the hood. On covered, rectangular barbecue grills, the spit is stationary and the firebed is moved up or down as necessary. *(For more information, see page 24.)*

Skewer Cooking

This cooking method is appropriate for any type of food, be it meat, fish, fowl, or vegetables. Skewer cooking can be used with any type of grill and requires only the purchase of long skewers onto which the food is threaded.

Here are several things to remember when skewer cooking:

- Grill kebabs over a solid bed of coals just slightly larger than the area occupied by the filled skewers.
- When threading skewers, leave a little space between chunks of food for more even cooking.
- When cooking kebabs over charcoal, place skewers on the grill about 4 inches above coals.
- To prevent flare-ups from dripping sauces and marinades, remove skewers from the grill before basting.
- For even cooking, turn skewers frequently.

Starting a Charcoal Fire

About 30 to 40 minutes before you intend to cook, prepare the firebox and start the fire. First, line the grill box with heavy-duty aluminum foil to aid in clean up. Place the grill away from shrubs, dry wood, and buildings. The fire can be started with a liquid, a solid, or an electric starter. If using a liquid starter, pile the number of briquets needed in a pyramid in the center of the firebox. The number of briquets needed will depend on the type of equipment you are using and the food you plan to cook. Generally speaking, to prepare a solid bed of coals in an 18- to 22-inch barbecue grill, you will need 25 to 35 briquets. (If you are making a divided bed of coals, add 5 to 10 briquets.) Use liquid starter according to label directions. Ignite briquets. Do not add fire starter after the fire has started.

If using an electric starter, be sure to remove it from the firebox after 8 to 10 minutes to prevent damage to the heating element.

For using grills other than charcoal burning, follow manufacturers' instructions.

Shape of the Fire

Coals can be arranged in a single layer in the firebox for uniform direct heat or they can be arranged on either side of the firebox for indirect heating.

Barbecue Basics

The choice of direct or indirect cooking is usually made based on the food to be cooked. Fast-cooking meat, flat meat, and poultry are usually grilled over direct heat; large cuts of meat and fatty foods are cooked over indirect heat with a drip pan dividing the coal bed. *(See page 4 for directions on how to make your own drip pan.)*

For spit roasting, coals are arranged in a solid, rectangular bed about 6 inches across and extending 3 to 4 inches beyond the food to be spit roasted. When spit roasting, add 5 or 6 briquets every ½ hour to maintain temperature level.

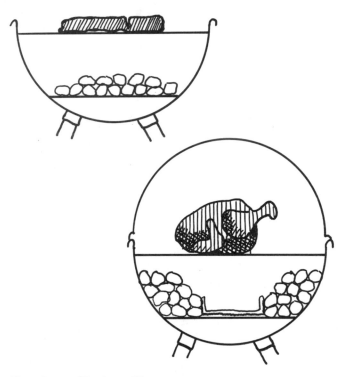

Ready — Start — Glow

Recipes in this book call for a cooking temperature of hot, medium-hot, or low. To determine the temperature of your fire, use the following tests:

HOT Coals are lightly covered with gray ash. Temperature reading on a thermometer is about 400° F. To test by hand, hold your hand over the grill and near the fire. If you can hold it only 2 to 3 seconds, coals are hot.

MEDIUM-HOT Coals are partially covered with ash as the fire begins to cool down. Temperature is about 350° F. Test by hand: 3 to 4 seconds.

LOW Coals are completely covered with thick, gray ash. Temperature is about 300° F. Test by hand: 4 to 5 seconds.

Grilling Timetable

The time required for grilling will vary depending on the type of barbecue equipment, temperature of the coals, and distance from the heat source. *For more information, see individual recipes.*

Beef Cuts	1 inch thick	
	Rare	8 to 12 minutes
	Medium	12 to 15 minutes
	Well-done	15 to 20 minutes
	1½ inches thick	
	Rare	10 to 15 minutes
	Medium	14 to 18 minutes
	Well-done	18 to 25 minutes
	2 inches thick	
	Rare	18 to 20 minutes
	Medium	25 to 30 minutes
	Well-done	45 to 60 minutes
	2½ inches thick	
	Rare	20 to 30 minutes
	Medium	35 to 45 minutes
	Well-done	60 to 75 minutes
Ground Beef	**Hamburgers**	
	Rare	10 to 12 minutes
	Medium	14 to 15 minutes
	Well-done	18 to 20 minutes
Lamb Chops and Steaks	**1 inch thick**	
	Medium-rare	8 to 16 minutes
	Well-done	18 to 25 minutes
	1½ inches thick	
	Medium-rare	8 to 16 minutes
	Well-done	20 to 30 minutes
Chicken	**Split or Cut-up**	
	25 to 45 minutes	
Ham Steaks	**1 inch thick**	
	30 to 35 minutes	
	1½ inches thick	
	35 to 45 minutes	
Fish Steaks	**1 inch thick**	
	6 to 9 minutes	
	1½ inches thick	
	8 to 12 minutes	

Beef

Marinated Beef Kebabs

Makes 6 servings

- ¼ cup vegetable oil
- 2 tablespoons cider vinegar
- 1 teaspoon celery salt
- 1 teaspoon onion salt
- ¾ teaspoon garlic salt
- ½ teaspoon salt
- ¾ teaspoon crushed leaf oregano
- ½ teaspoon black pepper
- 1 boneless beef shoulder *or* top round roast (about 2 pounds), cut in 1-inch cubes
- 6 medium mushroom caps
- 2 small zucchini, cut in ½-inch pieces

In a small saucepan, combine oil, vinegar, all salts, oregano, and pepper. Bring to boiling; remove from heat; let stand until cool. Place meat in a shallow pan or in a double plastic bag. Add mushrooms and zucchini. Pour marinade over meat and vegetables. Cover or seal. Refrigerate 4 to 6 hours, turning occasionally. Alternately thread meat and vegetables on 6 skewers. Grill over hot coals 10 to 15 minutes or until desired doneness, basting often with marinade.

Barbecued Short Ribs

Makes 4 servings

- 4 pounds beef short ribs
- 2 teaspoons salt
- ¼ teaspoon black pepper
- 1 can (8 ounces) tomato sauce
- ¼ cup catsup
- ⅓ cup packed brown sugar
- ¼ cup vinegar
- 2 tablespoons prepared mustard
- ½ cup chopped onion
- 1 clove garlic, minced
- 1 tablespoon chili powder

Place short ribs in a covered skillet. Grill slowly over low heat 1½ hours, turning occasionally. Season with salt and pepper. In a small saucepan, combine tomato sauce, catsup, brown sugar, vinegar, mustard, onion, garlic, and chili powder. Bring to boiling over medium heat, stirring frequently. Reduce heat; simmer 5 minutes. Dip ribs in sauce, coating all sides. Grill over low heat 20 to 30 minutes or until done, turning and brushing with sauce occasionally.

Spanish Olive Steak

Makes 4 servings

- 1 beef blade chuck steak (about 1½ inches thick, 3 to 3½ pounds)
- ½ cup sliced pimiento-stuffed olives
- 2 cloves garlic, sliced
- ⅓ cup lemon juice
- 3 tablespoons olive *or* vegetable oil
  Instant meat tenderizer
- 1 can (2 ounces) anchovy fillets, drained, optional
  Olive slices

Place steak in a shallow pan or in a double plastic bag. Top with olives. In a small bowl, combine garlic, lemon juice, and oil; pour over steak. Cover or seal. Refrigerate at least 8 hours, turning steak once. Drain marinade from steak; reserve marinade. Sprinkle on meat tenderizer following label directions. Grill about 4 inches from medium-hot coals 10 to 15 minutes on each side or until desired doneness. While steak is grilling, marinate anchovies in remaining olive oil marinade. Place steak on a heated serving platter. If desired, arrange anchovies in a criss-cross pattern over steak. Garnish with olive slices. Slice across the grain and serve.

Steak with Country Sauce

Makes 5 to 6 servings

- 1 teaspoon garlic salt
  Dash black pepper
- 1 beef flank steak (about 2 pounds)
- 2 slices bacon, diced
- 1 medium onion, chopped
- 1 tablespoon cider vinegar
- ½ cup grape jelly
- ½ cup catsup

Sprinkle garlic salt and pepper on both sides of steak. Place steak in a shallow pan or double plastic bag; set aside. In a large skillet, fry bacon until crisp; push to one side. Add onion; sauté until onion is golden. Add remaining ingredients; simmer until jelly melts and mixture is smooth, stirring occasionally. Pour sauce over steak. Cover or seal. Let stand 1 hour, turning steak once. Drain sauce from steak. Grill until desired doneness, brushing several times with sauce. Heat remaining sauce and serve with sliced steak.

Mustard Buttered Steaks

Makes 4 servings

  2 tablespoons butter, softened
  2 tablespoons prepared mustard
  4 T-bone steaks (about 1½ inches thick)

In a small dish, blend butter and mustard; set aside. Slash fat on edges of steaks to keep from curling. Grill over medium-hot coals 6 to 7 minutes on each side. Spread mustard butter over steak; grill 1 to 2 minutes. Turn steaks and spread the other side with mustard butter. Grill until desired doneness.

Tendered Beef

Makes 8 servings

  Instant meat tenderizer
  1 beef round or chuck roast (about 2 inches thick, 3 pounds)
  1 bottle (5 ounces) soy sauce
  ¼ cup packed brown sugar
  1 tablespoon lemon juice
  ¼ cup bourbon or brandy
  1 teaspoon Worcestershire sauce
  1½ cups water

Sprinkle meat tenderizer over roast following label directions. Place in a shallow pan or in a double plastic bag. In a small bowl, combine remaining ingredients; pour marinade over. Cover or seal. Refrigerate at least 6 hours, turning once. Drain marinade from roast; reserve marinade. Grill over hot coals 20 to 30 minutes or until desired doneness, turning and basting with marinade every 8 minutes.

Barbecued Top Sirloin Steak

Makes 4 servings

  1 beef top sirloin steak (1½ inches thick, 3 pounds)
  2 cups Burgundy wine
  1 teaspoon onion powder
  ¼ teaspoon garlic powder
  ¼ teaspoon black pepper

Place steak in a shallow pan or in a double plastic bag. Pour wine over steak; sprinkle on seasonings. Cover or seal. Refrigerate overnight, turning once. Drain marinade from steak; reserve marinade. Grill over medium-hot coals until desired doneness, basting occasionally with marinade.

Herb and Wine Barbecued Roast

Makes 8 servings

  1 beef round or shoulder roast (about 2½ inches thick, 3 pounds)
  2 cups dry red wine
  ½ cup vegetable oil
  2 tablespoons instant minced onion
  1½ tablespoons crushed leaf marjoram
  1 tablespoon salt
  ½ teaspoon minced garlic
  ¼ teaspoon black pepper

Place roast in a shallow pan or in a double plastic bag. In a small bowl, combine remaining ingredients; pour over meat. Cover or seal. Refrigerate about 24 hours, turning 2 or 3 times. Drain marinade from roast; reserve marinade. Grill over hot coals 20 to 30 minutes or until desired doneness, turning and basting with marinade every 8 minutes.

Mushroom Bacon Burgers

Makes 8 servings

  2 pounds lean ground beef
  1 can (8 ounces) mushroom stems and pieces, drained
  ¼ cup minced onion
  1 teaspoon salt
  ¼ teaspoon black pepper
  8 slices bacon, crisp-cooked and crumbled
  Butter Sauce, optional (recipe follows)
  8 hamburger rolls, split

In a large bowl, combine ground beef, mushrooms, onion, seasonings and bacon; blend well. Shape mixture into 8 patties. Chill 1 hour. Grill over medium-hot coals until desired doneness, brushing often with Butter Sauce, if desired. Serve on hamburger rolls.

Butter Sauce

Makes 1 cup

  ½ cup butter
  ½ cup chopped onion
  ½ cup catsup
  ¼ cup packed brown sugar
  1½ teaspoons chili powder
  1 teaspoon salt
  ⅛ teaspoon black pepper
  3 tablespoons Worcestershire sauce
  Dash hot pepper sauce

In a small saucepan, melt butter. Sauté onion until tender. Stir in catsup, brown sugar, chili powder, salt, pepper, and Worcestershire and hot pepper sauces. Simmer 5 minutes, stirring often.

Chuckwagon Steak

Makes 4 servings

- 1 beef flank steak (about 1 pound)
- 1 can (15 ounces) tomato sauce
- ¼ cup vegetable oil
- 1 small onion, chopped
- 2 tablespoons red wine vinegar
- 1 teaspoon brown sugar
- 1 teaspoon crushed red pepper flakes

Score both sides of steak with a sharp knife. In a small bowl, combine tomato sauce, oil, onion, vinegar, brown sugar, and red pepper flakes; blend well. Place steak in a shallow pan or in a double plastic bag. Pour sauce over steak. Cover or seal. Refrigerate at least 2 hours. Drain sauce from steak; reserve sauce. Grill over hot coals until desired doneness, turning and basting after 10 minutes. To serve, cut crosswise into thin slices. Heat remaining sauce and serve with steak.

Teriyaki Steak Sandwiches

Makes 12 servings

- Easy Hard Rolls (recipe follows) or 12 French baguettes
- 1 cup soy sauce
- ¾ cup vegetable oil
- 3 tablespoons chopped onion
- 1 clove garlic, crushed
- 3 tablespoons brown sugar
- 6 pounds beef skirt steaks

Prepare Easy Hard Rolls; set aside. In a large, flat baking dish or plastic container, combine soy sauce, vegetable oil, onion, garlic, and brown sugar; stir to dissolve sugar. Add steaks to marinade; turn to coat well. Refrigerate at least 2 hours. Drain marinade from steaks; reserve marinade. Grill steaks over hot coals 6 to 7 minutes on each side for medium well done. Cut into pieces and serve on sliced hard rolls or baguettes.

Easy Hard Rolls

Makes 12 rolls

- 1 package (¼ ounce) active dry yeast
- 1 cup warm water (110 to 115° F.)
- 2 tablespoons vegetable shortening
- 3 cups flour
- 2 tablespoons sugar
- 1¼ teaspoons salt
- 1 egg white mixed with 1 tablespoon water

In a small bowl, sprinkle yeast over water; set aside to soften. In a large mixing bowl, cut shortening into flour, sugar, and salt until consistency of fine crumbs. Add yeast; stir until a soft dough forms. Cover and let rise in a warm, draft-free place for 20 minutes. Divide dough into 12 portions. Flatten each portion into a 4 x 3-inch rectangle. Roll up from long side; pinch edges to seal. Preheat oven to 375° F. Place rolls about 3 inches apart on a greased baking sheet. Brush with egg white. Cover and let rise for 1 hour. Bake 25 to 30 minutes or until golden. Cool on a wire rack. Split each roll lengthwise.

Wine Marinated Blade Steak

Makes 3 to 4 servings

- ½ cup red wine vinegar
- ½ cup water
- 1 medium onion, chopped
- 1½ teaspoons sugar
- 1 teaspoon salt
- ½ teaspoon crushed leaf basil
- ¼ teaspoon celery seed
- ⅛ teaspoon black pepper
- 1 beef chuck blade steak (¾ to 1 inch thick, 2 pounds)

In a small saucepan, combine vinegar, water, onion, sugar, salt, basil, celery seed, and pepper; blend well. Simmer 10 minutes, stirring occasionally; cool. Place steak in a shallow pan or in a double plastic bag. Pour marinade over steak. Cover or seal. Refrigerate 6 to 8 hours, turning once. Drain marinade from steak; reserve marinade. Grill steak over hot coals until desired doneness, basting often.

Italian Hamburger Kebabs

Makes 6 servings

- 1½ pounds lean ground beef
- 1 cup soft bread crumbs
- 1 egg, lightly beaten
- 2 tablespoons grated Parmesan cheese
- 1¼ teaspoons salt
- 1 teaspoon Italian seasoning
- 1 can (8 ounces) whole mushrooms, drained
- Vegetable oil
- Sliced Italian bread, optional

In a small bowl, combine all ingredients, except mushrooms, oil, and bread; blend well. Shape into 1½-inch balls. Alternately thread meatballs and mushrooms on skewers. Brush on oil. Grill over hot coals 6 to 10 minutes, turning to cook all sides. Serve on sliced Italian bread, if desired.

Beef

Hawaiian Burgers

Makes 8 servings

2 pounds lean ground beef
½ cup minced onion
2 teaspoons salt
¼ teaspoon black pepper
2 eggs
3 tablespoons prepared mustard
3 tablespoons catsup
1½ tablespoons soy sauce
8 pineapple slices, drained and heated

In a large bowl, combine ground beef, onion, salt, pepper, and eggs; blend well. Shape into 8 large patties; set aside. In a small bowl, combine mustard, catsup, and soy sauce; blend well. Brush mustard mixture over hamburger patties. Grill over low heat until desired doneness. Serve each topped with a pineapple slice.

Stuffing Stuffed Burgers

Makes 6 servings

1½ pounds lean ground beef
1½ teaspoons salt
1 cup seasoned stuffing mix
1 medium onion, grated
¼ cup butter *or* margarine
2 tablespoons lemon juice
¼ teaspoon black pepper
Dash cayenne pepper

In a medium bowl, combine ground beef and salt; blend well. Divide into 12 equal portions. Flatten each portion between pieces of waxed paper into 5-inch patties. Do not remove patties from waxed paper. In a small bowl, combine remaining ingredients; blend well. Divide stuffing mixture among 6 of the hamburger patties. Top each with a second patty; press edges together to seal. Remove from waxed paper. Grill over medium-hot coals until desired doneness.

Cookout Burgers

Makes 6 servings

1½ pounds lean ground beef
1 cup instant nonfat dry milk
1 teaspoon salt
1 egg
1 tablespoon instant minced onion
6 hamburger rolls

In a large bowl, combine all ingredients, except rolls; blend well. Shape into 6 large, flat patties.

Grill patties over medium-hot coals until desired doneness. Serve on hamburger rolls.

Variation

Shape beef mixture into 18 balls. Alternately thread meatballs on a skewer along with tomato and green pepper wedges, mushrooms, and onions. Grill over medium-hot coals or hot coals, wrapped in heavy-duty aluminum foil, until desired doneness.

Grill Top Pizza

Makes 4 servings

1 pound lean ground beef
1 teaspoon salt
1 can (8 ounces) refrigerated crescent rolls, separated
1 jar (8 ounces) pizza sauce
1 medium onion, sliced
1 can (4 ounces) mushroom stems and pieces, drained
⅓ cup pitted ripe olives, sliced
4 ounces mozzarella cheese, shredded (1 cup)

Brown ground beef in a skillet on the grill; drain on paper towels. Sprinkle on salt. In the same skillet, arrange crescent roll dough in a circle; press edges together to form a crust. Spread half of the pizza sauce over the dough. Spoon ground beef over pizza sauce. Top with onion, mushrooms, and olives. Pour remaining sauce over all. Sprinkle on cheese. Cover tightly with aluminum foil. Grill over medium-hot coals 20 to 30 minutes or until crust is golden brown.

Pizza Patties

Makes 4 servings

1 pound lean ground beef
¾ cup cracker crumbs
½ cup grated mozzarella cheese
1 small onion, minced
1 clove garlic, minced
¼ teaspoon crushed leaf oregano
Salt and pepper
1 egg, lightly beaten
¼ cup tomato paste
¼ cup red wine
4 hamburger rolls

In a large bowl, combine all ingredients, except rolls; blend well. Shape into 4 patties. Grill over hot coals until desired doneness. Serve on hamburger rolls.

Bean and Pepper Enchiladas

Makes 8 servings

- 2 pounds lean ground beef
- 1 medium onion, chopped
- 2 teaspoons salt
- 2 cans (16 ounces each) kidney beans, drained; reserve ½ cup liquid
- 2 ounces Cheddar cheese, shredded (½ cup)
- 1 clove garlic, minced
- 1 can (16 ounces) tomatoes, undrained
- 1 can (15 ounces) tomato sauce
- 1 can (4 ounces) chopped green chilies, drained
- 1 package (10 ounces) corn tortillas

Brown ground beef and onion in a large saucepan or Dutch oven directly on grill, if desired; drain fat. Sprinkle on salt; set aside. In a small saucepan, combine beans and ½ cup reserved bean liquid; mash with a fork; heat through. Add cheese and garlic to beans; blend well. Add remaining bean liquid, tomatoes, tomato sauce, and chilies to ground beef. Cover and cook 30 minutes. Dip 2 or 3 tortillas at a time into meat mixture to soften. Remove to waxed paper. Spoon about 3 tablespoons bean mixture down center of each tortilla; fold 2 sides in, overlapping in center and enclosing bean mixture. Tear off a piece of heavy-duty aluminum foil 2 inches longer than diameter of skillet; pierce several times with a fork. Place foil over meat mixture in skillet. Place filled tortillas on foil; cover and cook over low heat 15 to 20 minutes. Remove tortillas and foil. Serve with hot beef mixture.

Teriyaki Hamburger Steak

Makes 8 servings

- 2 pounds lean ground beef
- 1 teaspoon salt
- ¼ teaspoon black pepper
- 2 tablespoons minced parsley
  Bottled teriyaki sauce
  Green onions, sliced diagonally
- 8 hamburger rolls

In a large bowl, combine ground beef, salt, pepper, parsley, and 2 tablespoons teriyaki sauce; mix lightly. Shape into 8 1¼-inch-thick oval patties. Brush on teriyaki sauce. Grill over medium-hot coals until desired doneness, brushing occasionally with teriyaki sauce. Carefully remove steaks from grill with two spatulas. Serve on hamburger rolls topped with sliced green onions.

Vegetable Stuffed Burgers

Makes 4 servings

- 8 ground steak patties, about ¼ inch thick
- 8 green pepper strips
- 4 onion rings
- 4 slices tomato
- 4 slices American cheese
  Salt and pepper
  Prepared mustard
- 4 hamburger rolls

On a large square of heavy-duty aluminum foil, place 1 ground steak patty. Top with 2 green pepper strips, 1 onion ring, 1 tomato slice, and 1 cheese slice. Season to taste with salt, pepper, and mustard. Top with a second patty; press edges together to seal. Repeat for remaining steak patties. Wrap each securely in foil. Grill over low heat 10 minutes on each side. Serve on hamburger rolls.

Stuffed Green Peppers

Makes 6 servings

- 1½ pounds lean ground beef
- 2 tablespoons minced onion
- 2 tablespoons minced green pepper
- 1 can (15 ounces) tomato sauce
- ½ cup uncooked instant quick-cooking rice
- 4 small tomatoes, peeled and quartered
- 1 cup water
  Salt and pepper
- 6 medium green peppers, tops removed, seeded
  Tomato sauce

Brown ground beef and onion in a skillet on the grill; drain fat. Add minced green pepper, tomato sauce, rice, tomatoes, water, and salt and pepper to taste; blend well. Simmer 15 minutes, stirring occasionally. Stuff peppers with beef mixture. Place filled peppers in a large baking pan. Top each with a spoonful of tomato sauce. Cover pan with aluminum foil. Grill over indirect heat 40 to 50 minutes or until peppers are tender.

Pork and Lamb

Barbecued Pork Loin Roast

Makes 6 to 8 servings

   1 boneless pork loin roast (3 to 4 pounds)
     Salt and pepper
   ¼ cup sugar
   ⅓ cup catsup
   3 tablespoons vinegar
   1 tablespoon prepared mustard
   1 tablespoon vegetable oil

Season roast with salt and pepper to taste. Cover loosely with a piece of heavy-duty aluminum foil. Grill over medium-hot coals for 1 hour. While roast is grilling, combine remaining ingredients in a small saucepan. Bring to boiling; reduce heat. Simmer 5 minutes, stirring often. After 1 hour, baste roast with barbecue sauce; continue basting every 15 minutes until roast is done, about 1½ to 2 hours (170° F. on a meat thermometer inserted in the thickest part of the roast).

Lamb and Vegetable Kebabs

Makes 6 servings

   1 carton (8 ounces) dairy sour cream *or* plain yogurt
   2 tablespoons lemon juice
   1 teaspoon olive *or* vegetable oil
   1 large onion, minced
   ½ cup snipped mint leaves *or* 4 teaspoons dried mint
   2 tablespoons chopped parsley
   ¼ teaspoon cayenne pepper
     Salt and pepper
   2 pounds boneless leg of lamb, cubed
  18 cherry tomatoes
   2 green peppers, cut in chunks
  18 pearl onions, peeled
  18 medium mushrooms
     Fluffy hot rice

In a small bowl, combine sour cream, lemon juice, oil, onion, mint, parsley, cayenne, and salt and pepper to taste; blend well. Place cubed lamb in a shallow pan or in a double plastic bag. Pour sauce over lamb. Cover or seal. Refrigerate at least 4 hours, turning occasionally. Remove from refrigerator 2 hours before grilling. Remove lamb cubes from sauce. Alternately thread lamb, tomatoes, peppers, onions, and mushrooms on skewers. Grill over hot coals about 5 minutes on each side or until lamb is desired doneness. Serve with rice.

Grilled Ham Steaks with Honey Glaze

Makes 4 to 6 servings

   3 tablespoons honey
   1 tablespoon Worcestershire sauce
   1 tablespoon dry mustard
   ¾ teaspoon ground ginger
     Dash black pepper
   1 center-cut ham slice (1 inch thick, about 2 pounds)

In a small bowl, combine honey, Worcestershire sauce, dry mustard, ginger, and pepper; blend well; set aside. Grease grill lightly. Place ham on grill 4 to 6 inches over low heat. Grill about 20 minutes, or until browned, turning and basting with honey glaze.

Variation

Brown Sugar Glaze: Combine 1 cup ginger ale and ½ cup brown sugar. Top ham with pineapple rings and cherries, if desired.

Orange Barbecued Ribs

Makes 3 to 4 servings

   3 pounds country-style pork spareribs
     Salt and pepper
   ⅓ cup orange marmalade
   ¼ cup lemon juice
   ¼ cup soy sauce
   1 clove garlic, minced
   2 teaspoons cornstarch
   2 tablespoons water

On a large double thickness of heavy-duty aluminum foil, arrange the spareribs in a single layer. Season lightly with salt and pepper. Fold foil up and over ribs; seal edge and ends with a double fold. Place on grill about 4 inches from coals. Grill about 45 minutes over medium-hot coals, turning once. While ribs are grilling, combine orange marmalade, lemon juice, soy sauce, and garlic in a small saucepan. Dissolve cornstarch in water; add to marmalade mixture. Cook over medium heat until thickened, stirring constantly. Remove ribs and foil from grill; discard foil. Dip ribs in sauce to coat well. Grill 5 minutes on each side directly on grill.

Pork/Lamb

Grilled Precooked Whole Ham

    1 precooked whole ham (Allow ¾ pound per person)
    Pineapple rings, optional
    Maraschino cherry halves, optional

Remove any rind from outside and score fat in a diamond pattern, using a sharp knife. Grill over indirect heat 9 minutes per pound or until heated through. For best results, use a meat thermometer. After the first ½ hour, baste with Honey or Brown Sugar Glaze (recipes on page 15) or use your favorite glaze. If desired, garnish with pineapple rings and cherries about 15 minutes before the end of cooking time and brush with glaze.

Note: If using a partially cooked ham, such as smoked or cured, heat to an internal temperature of 160° F.

Western Barbecued Ribs

Makes 4 to 5 servings

    4 pounds country-style pork spareribs, cut in serving
        pieces
    1 teaspoon salt
    ¼ teaspoon black pepper
    ⅔ cup catsup
    3 tablespoons cider vinegar
    1 tablespoon soy sauce
    2 tablespoons instant minced onion
    1 tablespoon chili powder
    ¼ teaspoon garlic powder

Sprinkle both sides of ribs with salt and pepper. Fold foil up and over ribs; seal edge and ends with a double fold. Place on grill about 4 inches from coals. Grill about 45 minutes over medium-hot coals, turning once. While ribs are grilling, combine remaining ingredients in a small bowl; blend well. Brush generously over ribs. Grill over hot coals 5 minutes on each side.

Grilled Smoked Ham Steak

Makes 3 to 4 servings

    2 uncooked smoked ham steaks, 1 inch thick
    1 cup apple cider
    3 tablespoons brown sugar
    1 tablespoon dry mustard
    3 whole cloves, crushed

Trim fat from ham. Score edges at 1-inch intervals. Place ham in a large skillet. Cover with boiling water. Bring to a boil; parboil 5 minutes; drain. In a small bowl, combine remaining ingredients; blend well. Pour over ham steaks in skillet; let

stand 15 minutes. Drain marinade from steaks; reserve marinade. Grease grill with fat trimmings. Grill over medium-hot coals until browned on both sides, turning and basting often with marinade until done (160° F. on a meat thermometer).

Pork Sausage and Chili Scrambled Eggs

Makes 3 to 4 servings

    6 eggs
    ¼ cup half-and-half *or* milk
    1 teaspoon salt
    ¼ teaspoon chili powder
        Dash black pepper
    3 tablespoons butter *or* margarine
    6 to 8 precooked sausage links

In a medium bowl, combine eggs, half-and-half, salt, chili powder, pepper, and butter; beat lightly until blended. Pour into a greased aluminum foil pan. Place pan on grill along with sausage links. Grill over low heat 10 to 15 minutes, turning sausages and stirring eggs frequently.

Pineapple Glazed Spareribs

Makes 6 servings

    4 to 5 pounds country-style spareribs
    1½ teaspoons salt
    ½ teaspoon garlic salt
    ½ cup apple *or* currant jelly
    1 can (29 ounces) sliced pineapple, drained;
        reserve liquid
    ⅓ cup honey
    1 tablespoon soy sauce
    ½ teaspoon ground ginger
    ¼ teaspoon red food coloring, optional

On a large double thickness of heavy-duty aluminum foil, arrange the spareribs in a single layer. Combine salts in a small dish; sprinkle evenly over ribs. Fold foil up and over ribs; seal edge and ends with a double fold. Place on grill about 4 inches from coals. Grill about 1 hour, turning once. While ribs are grilling, combine jelly and reserved pineapple liquid, honey, soy sauce, ginger, and food coloring, if desired, in a medium saucepan. Bring to boiling over low heat; stirring frequently. Simmer 5 minutes, stirring often. Remove ribs and foil from grill; discard foil. Dip ribs in sauce to coat well. Place ribs directly on grill. Grill 5 minutes and serve.

Lemon Marinated Kebabs

Makes 8 servings

- ¼ cup olive or vegetable oil
- ⅓ cup lemon juice
- 2 teaspoons salt
- 1 teaspoon black pepper
- 2 cloves garlic, minced
- 1 teaspoon crushed rosemary leaves
- 1 boneless leg or shoulder of lamb (2 to 2½ pounds) cut in 1-inch cubes
- 1 large onion, cut in chunks
- 2 large green peppers, cut in chunks
- 16 whole cherry tomatoes
- 32 pitted ripe olives

In a small bowl, combine olive oil, lemon juice, salt, pepper, garlic, and rosemary; blend well. Place lamb cubes, onion, and green pepper in a pan just large enough to hold all or in a double plastic bag. Pour marinade over meat and vegetables; toss lightly to coat. Cover or seal. Refrigerate at least 4 hours, turning occasionally. Drain marinade from meat and vegetables; reserve marinade. Alternately thread meat, onion, green peppers, tomatoes, and ripe olives on 16 skewers. Grill over hot coals, turning and basting often with marinade, until meat is no longer pink inside.

Leg of Lamb

Makes 6 servings

- 1 leg of lamb (about 8 pounds) Salt and pepper
- 2 cloves garlic, cut in slivers

Season leg of lamb with salt and pepper to taste. Make several slits in lamb with a sharp knife. Insert a garlic sliver in each slit. Place lamb in center of grill over indirect heat. Cook about 2 hours or until for well done (180° F. on a meat thermometer inserted in the thickest portion).

Orange Marmalade Leg of Lamb

Makes 6 to 8 servings

- 3 tablespoons teriyaki sauce
- ⅔ cup orange juice
- 1 clove garlic, minced
- 1 leg of lamb (about 8 pounds), butterflied
- ½ cup orange marmalade

In a small bowl, combine teriyaki sauce, orange juice, and garlic; blend well. Place lamb in a shallow pan or in a double plastic bag. Pour sauce over lamb. Cover or seal. Refrigerate at least 4 hours, basting occasionally with sauce. Grill lamb over hot coals about 1¼ hours or until desired doneness, basting occasionally with marinade. During the last half hour of cooking, stir marmalade into marinade and continue basting.

Ground Lamb Kebabs

Makes 6 servings

- ¾ cup instant minced onion, rehydrated; divided
- ¾ cup water
- 2 tablespoons butter or margarine
- 2 pounds lean ground lamb
- 1 egg, lightly beaten
- 2 tablespoons parsley flakes
- 1¾ teaspoons salt
- ¾ teaspoon ground cumin
- ⅛ teaspoon black pepper
- 12 whole cherry tomatoes
  Rice Pilaf (recipe on page 40), optional

Rehydrate onion in water 10 minutes. In a small skillet, melt butter. Add half of the onion; sauté 4 minutes. In a large mixing bowl, combine sautéed onion, lamb, egg, parsley flakes, salt, cumin, and pepper; blend just until mixed. Shape meat mixture into 2 x ¾-inch oval patties. Alternately thread meat and tomatoes on 6 skewers. Grill over hot coals 10 to 12 minutes or until desired doneness, turning often. Sprinkle kebabs with remaining onion. Serve with Rice Pilaf, if desired.

Scalloped Potatoes and Ham

Makes 8 servings

- 6 medium potatoes, peeled and sliced
- ¼ cup chopped onion
- 1 cup diced ham
- 1 can (10¾ ounces) cream of mushroom soup, undiluted
- ½ cup milk
- 1 teaspoon salt
- ⅛ teaspoon black pepper

Grease an 11 x 7-inch aluminum foil pan; set aside. In a bowl, combine sliced potatoes, onion, and ham; mix lightly. In a small bowl, combine soup, milk, salt, and pepper; blend well. Blend into potato mixture. Transfer to prepared pan. Grill, uncovered, over medium-hot coals about 1 hour or until potatoes are tender.

Variety Meats

Stuffed Frankfurters

Makes 4 servings

    4 frankfurters
      Mustard
    1 slice American cheese, cut in 4 strips
    8 tablespoons sauerkraut
    4 strips bacon
    4 frankfurter rolls

Slit frankfurters lengthwise to make a pocket. Brush with mustard. Place a strip of cheese and 2 tablespoons sauerkraut in each slit. Wrap a strip of bacon spiral-fashion around each hot dog; fasten with toothpicks. Grill over hot coals until bacon is crisp. Serve on frankfurter rolls.

Franks with Pepper Relish

Makes 8 to 10 servings

    2 tablespoons vegetable oil
    2 medium onions, sliced
    1 large green pepper, cut in thin strips
    1 large red pepper, cut in thin strips
    ¼ cup water
    1 teaspoon salt
    ¼ teaspoon Italian seasoning
    1 pound frankfurters (8 to 10 per pound)
    8 to 10 5-inch pieces French bread

In a large skillet heat oil; sauté onions until tender. Add green and red pepper strips; cook slowly for 15 minutes, stirring frequently. Add water, salt, and Italian seasoning. Bring to boiling; reduce heat. Cover and simmer 10 minutes. While relish is cooking, grill frankfurters over hot coals 8 to 10 minutes, turning occasionally. Cut through centers of bread to open but not separate. Place frankfurters on bread and top with pepper relish.

Grilled Hot Dogs

Makes 8 to 10 servings

    1 pound frankfurters
    8 to 10 frankfurter buns
      Catsup, mustard, relish, etc.

Grill frankfurters over medium-hot coals 12 to 15 minutes or until heated through. Top with your favorite condiments. Serve on frankfurter buns.

Brats 'n Kraut

Makes 4 servings

    1 cup beer
    4 bratwursts
    1 can (16 ounces) sauerkraut
    4 brat buns or hard rolls, split

Pour beer into an 11 x 7-inch pan. Place pan in center of grill. Brown bratwursts on side of grill over hot coals, turning with tongs until light brown. Place brats in beer. Cover and cook 25 minutes or until brats are done. About 15 minutes before end of cooking time, empty sauerkraut into a small pan. Place pan on grill and heat sauerkraut through, about 15 minutes. Serve bratwursts on buns or hard rolls topped with sauerkraut.

Sausage Italiano

Makes 4 servings

    1½ tablespoons vegetable oil
      2 large green peppers, cut in 1½-inch strips
    ¼ cup boiling water
    ½ teaspoon salt
      4 Italian sausages
      2 teaspoons vegetable oil
      1 medium onion, chopped
      1 clove garlic, minced
      1 cup diced fresh tomatoes or 1 cup canned
        tomatoes
      1 teaspoon sugar
      1 teaspoon salt
    ¼ teaspoon black pepper
    ¼ teaspoon crushed leaf basil
      4 hard rolls, split

In a large skillet, heat 1½ tablespoons oil. Add green peppers; sauté until tender-crisp. Add boiling water and salt. Cover and simmer 20 minutes or until tender; drain peppers; set aside. Grill sausages over direct heat 10 minutes or until lightly browned, turning to brown evenly on all sides. Move sausages to center of grill directly over drip pan. Cover and cook 25 to 30 minutes or until done. While sausages are grilling, heat 2 teaspoons oil in a medium saucepan; sauté onion and garlic until tender. Add tomatoes, sugar, salt, pepper, and basil. Bring to boiling. Simmer, uncovered, 25 minutes or until thickened. Add drained green peppers; blend well. Place sausages in hard rolls. Top with green pepper-tomato sauce and serve.

Grilled Hot Dogs
German Potato Salad, 44

Variety Meats

German Bratwurst

Makes 4 servings

- 2 tablespoons vegetable oil
- 4 bratwursts
- 1½ cups chopped onions
- 1 can (12 ounces) beer
- 2 tablespoons butter *or* margarine
- ½ teaspoon onion salt
- 4 bratwurst *or* frankfurter rolls
- ½ cup grated sharp Cheddar cheese
- 4 slices bacon, crisp-fried and crumbled

In a skillet, heat oil. Brown bratwursts on all sides. Add onions and beer. Simmer, uncovered, 20 to 30 minutes. In a small bowl, combine butter and onion salt; blend well. Spread onion butter on rolls. Slit each bratwurst lengthwise to within ½ inch of each end. Place bratwursts in rolls. Top with onion, cheese, and bacon bits. Place each on a piece of heavy-duty aluminum foil. Bring foil up and over sandwich; seal tightly. Grill 3 to 5 minutes or until cheese melts.

Knackwurst Bavarian

Makes 4 servings

- 4 slices bacon, crisp-cooked and crumbled; reserve drippings
- ½ cup chopped onion
- 4 cups shredded red cabbage
- 1 tart apple, peeled, cored, and chopped
- 1 tablespoon sugar
- ½ teaspoon salt
- ⅛ teaspoon black pepper
- ¼ teaspoon caraway seed
- 3 tablespoons cider vinegar
- 4 knackwursts

In a large skillet, heat reserved bacon drippings. Add onion; sauté until onion is tender. Add cabbage, apple, sugar, salt, pepper, and caraway seed; blend well. Cover and simmer 10 minutes. Add vinegar; blend well; set aside. Brown knackwursts on grill on all sides. Place in an 11 x 7-inch aluminum pan. Top with cabbage mixture. Cover and place on grill. Grill 15 to 20 minutes or until knackwursts are done and cabbage is tender. Top with bacon and serve.

Chicken Livers and Mushrooms

Makes 4 servings

- 1 pound chicken livers, rinsed and halved
- 2 tablespoons butter *or* margarine, melted
- ¼ cup dry white wine
- ½ cup dry bread crumbs
- ¼ teaspoon onion salt
- 4 large mushrooms, quartered
- 2 large tomatoes, cut in wedges
- ½ cup French dressing

In a medium bowl, combine livers, butter, and wine; stir lightly. Cover and refrigerate 30 minutes. In a small bowl, combine bread crumbs and onion salt. Drain liquid from livers. Roll in crumb mixture to coat well. Alternately thread livers, mushrooms, and tomato wedges on four 10-inch skewers. Brush with French dressing. Grill over medium coals 15 minutes or until livers are just browned, turning and basting once. Be careful not to burn livers.

Texas Liver and Onion Kebabs

Makes 4 servings

- Texas Barbecue Sauce (recipe follows)
- 1 pound beef, lamb, or calf's liver, thinly sliced
- 4 slices bacon
- 1 sweet red pepper, seeded and cubed
- 1 sweet green pepper, seeded and cubed
- 8 small white onions, peeled and parboiled

Prepare Texas Barbecue Sauce; set aside. Cut liver into 1-inch strips. Place bacon on a flat surface; top each piece with 1 or 2 strips liver. Alternately thread liver and bacon accordian-style onto skewers along with peppers and onions. Brush with barbecue sauce. Grill over hot coals 15 minutes or just until bacon is crisp, turning and brushing often with sauce. Do not overcook.

Texas Barbecue Sauce

Makes about 1½ cups

- ½ cup cold coffee
- ½ cup Worcestershire sauce
- ½ cup catsup
- ¼ cup cider vinegar
- ¼ cup packed brown sugar
- 1 tablespoon chili powder
- 1½ teaspoons salt
- ½ cup chopped onion
- 2 teaspoons minced jalapeno peppers
- ½ teaspoon garlic powder

In a saucepan, combine all ingredients. Simmer, uncovered, 30 minutes, stirring frequently.

Poultry

Chicken Kebabs with Pineapple

Makes 3 to 4 servings

    1 can (16 ounces) pineapple chunks, drained;
       reserve juice
    4 teaspoons soy sauce
    ½ teaspoon grated fresh gingerroot
    2 green peppers, cut in chunks
    4 whole chicken breasts, skinned and boned

In a small bowl, combine reserved pineapple juice, soy sauce, and gingerroot; blend well. Cut chicken breasts into large chunks. Alternately thread chicken, peppers, and pineapple chunks onto skewers. Place skewers in a shallow pan. Pour marinade over skewers. Let stand 1 hour. Drain marinade from kebabs; reserve marinade. Grill kebabs over medium-hot coals about 20 minutes or until chicken is tender, turning and basting often.

Stuffed Chicken Breasts

Makes 8 servings

    8 whole chicken breasts, boned
      Salt and pepper
    1 package (8 ounces) seasoned croutons
    1 can (10¾ ounces) cream of mushroom soup,
      undiluted, divided
    1 can (7 ounces) crab meat, drained and flaked
  ¼ cup chopped green pepper
    1 egg, lightly beaten
    1 tablespoon lemon juice
    2 teaspoons Worcestershire sauce
    1 teaspoon prepared mustard
  ¼ teaspoon salt
  ¼ cup vegetable oil
  ¼ teaspoon onion juice
    1 teaspoon Kitchen Bouquet

Sprinkle inside of chicken breasts with salt and pepper to taste. In a bowl, combine croutons, ½ can of the soup, crab meat, green pepper, egg, lemon juice, Worcestershire sauce, mustard, and ¼ teaspoon salt; blend well. Divide stuffing among chicken breasts. Roll breasts up; secure with skewers. Grill stuffed breasts over medium-hot coals 30 minutes. While breasts are cooking, combine remaining ½ can soup, oil, onion juice, Kitchen Bouquet, and a dash of pepper in a small bowl; blend well. Baste chicken with sauce. Grill 15 minutes, turning and basting frequently.

Onion Barbecue Chicken

Makes 8 servings

    1 can (10¾ ounces) onion soup, undiluted
  ½ cup catsup
  ¼ cup vegetable oil
  ¼ cup vinegar
    2 tablespoons brown sugar
    1 tablespoon Worcestershire sauce
  ⅛ teaspoon hot pepper sauce
    2 cloves garlic, minced
    2 broiler-fryer chickens (2½ to 3 pounds each), cut up

In a medium saucepan, combine soup, catsup, oil, vinegar, brown sugar, and Worcestershire and hot pepper sauces. Cook over medium heat until hot, stirring often. Place chicken in a shallow pan or in a double plastic bag. Pour sauce over chicken. Cover or seal. Refrigerate several hours or overnight. Drain sauce from chicken; reserve sauce. Grill chicken over hot coals about 15 minutes, turning to brown both sides. Brush with sauce. Grill 30 minutes or until chicken is tender, turning and basting often.

Orange Teriyaki Chicken

Makes 8 servings

    1 can (6 ounces) frozen orange juice concentrate,
      thawed
  ¼ cup soy sauce
    2 tablespoons chopped onion
    1 tablespoon vegetable oil
  ½ teaspoon ground ginger
  ½ teaspoon hot pepper sauce
    2 broiler-fryer chickens (2½ to 3 pounds each), cut up

In a small bowl, combine orange juice concentrate, soy sauce, onion, oil, ginger, and hot pepper sauce; blend well. Place chicken in a shallow pan or in a double plastic bag. Pour marinade over chicken. Cover or seal. Refrigerate at least 2 hours, turning once. Drain marinade from chicken; reserve marinade. Grill chicken over medium-hot coals about 45 minutes or until tender, turning and basting often.

Poultry

Orange and Beer Chicken

Makes 6 to 8 servings

1 can (12 ounces) beer
1 teaspoon salt
¼ teaspoon seasoned pepper
2 tablespoons lemon juice
Generous dash hot pepper sauce
½ teaspoon orange extract
1 teaspoon grated orange peel
1 tablespoon brown sugar
1 tablespoon dark molasses
2 broiler-fryer chickens (2½ to 3 pounds each), halved

In a small bowl, combine beer, salt, pepper, lemon juice, hot pepper sauce, orange extract and peel, brown sugar, and molasses; blend well. Place chicken in a shallow pan or in a double plastic bag. Pour marinade over chicken. Cover or seal. Refrigerate several hours or overnight. Drain marinade from chicken; reserve marinade. Grill chicken over hot coals about 45 minutes or until tender, turning and basting often.

Grilled Lemon Chicken

Makes 4 to 6 servings

½ cup lemon or lime juice
½ cup butter or margarine, melted
1 teaspoon crushed leaf thyme
¼ teaspoon hot pepper sauce
Salt and pepper
2 broiler-fryer chickens (2½ to 3 pounds each), quartered

In a small bowl, combine lemon juice, butter, thyme, and hot pepper sauce; blend well. Sprinkle salt and pepper to taste on chickens. Grill chickens over hot coals about 45 minutes or until tender, turning and basting often. Serve with remaining lemon butter.

Golden Glazed Chicken

Makes 4 servings

¼ cup butter or margarine
1 can (30 ounces) spiced peaches, drained; reserve syrup
2 tablespoons vinegar
1 teaspoon soy sauce
2 tablespoons prepared mustard
2 tablespoons minced onion
1 teaspoon salt
1 broiler-fryer chicken (2½ to 3 pounds), quartered

In a small saucepan, combine butter, 1½ cups reserved peach syrup, vinegar, soy sauce, mustard, onion, and salt. Bring to boiling, stirring often. Place chicken in a shallow pan. Pour peach mixture over chicken. Let stand 30 to 40 minutes. Drain marinade from chicken; reserve marinade. Grill chicken over hot coals about 45 minutes or until tender, turning and basting often. Serve with warmed spiced peaches.

Cranberry Barbecued Chicken

Makes 8 servings

1 can (8 ounces) jellied cranberry sauce
4 teaspoons soy sauce
2 teaspoons lemon juice
½ teaspoon ground ginger
16 chicken legs or thighs

In a saucepan, combine cranberry sauce, soy sauce, lemon juice, and ginger; blend well. Cook over medium heat 10 minutes, stirring occasionally. Arrange chicken on a large double thickness of heavy-duty aluminum foil. Grill over hot coals about 15 minutes, turning often. Baste with cranberry mixture. Grill 30 to 35 minutes or until tender, turning and basting often.

Island Broiled Chicken

Makes 6 to 8 servings

½ cup soy sauce
¼ cup water
⅓ cup vegetable oil
2 tablespoons instant minced onion
2 tablespoons sesame seed
1 tablespoon sugar
1 teaspoon ground ginger
¾ teaspoon salt
½ teaspoon instant minced garlic
⅛ teaspoon cayenne pepper
2 broiler-fryer chickens (2½ to 3 pounds each), quartered

In a small bowl, combine soy sauce, water, oil, onion, sesame seed, sugar, ginger, salt, garlic, and pepper; blend well. Place chicken in a shallow pan or in a double plastic bag. Pour marinade over chicken. Cover or seal. Refrigerate 8 hours or overnight, turning occasionally. Drain marinade from chicken; reserve marinade. Grill chicken over hot coals 45 minutes or until tender, turning and basting.

Poultry

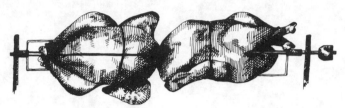

Soy Glazed Cornish Hens

Makes 4 servings

> 4 Cornish game hens (1 to 1½ pounds each)
> Salt and pepper
> ½ cup soy sauce
> ½ cup dry sherry
> 1 tablespoon lemon juice
> ¼ cup vegetable oil
> 1 clove garlic, crushed

Sprinkle cavities of hens with salt and pepper. Secure neck skin to backs of chickens with skewers. Press wings over breasts and tie with heavy string. Tie legs together; tie legs to tail. Insert spit rod crosswise through each hen just below the breastbone, leaving about 1 inch between hens. Secure with holding forks. Test balance; attach to spit. Turn on motor. Grill over drip pan surrounded by medium-hot coals about 45 minutes. In a bowl, combine soy sauce, sherry, lemon juice, oil, and garlic. Brush on hens. Grill 15 minutes or until leg joints move easily, basting often with sauce.

Stuffed Chicken

Makes 4 servings

> 4 tablespoons butter or margarine, divided
> ½ cup shredded zucchini
> ¾ cup water
> ½ package (6½ ounces) stuffing mix with rice
> ½ cup shredded mozzarella cheese
> 1 teaspoon grated lemon peel
> 2 tablespoons lemon juice
> ½ teaspoon crushed leaf basil
> 1 roasting chicken (4 to 4½ pounds)
> 1 teaspoon salt

In a large saucepan, melt 1 tablespoon butter. Sauté zucchini until tender. Stir in water and seasonings from stuffing mix. Bring to boiling; remove from heat. Add stuffing mix; toss lightly with a fork until moistened. Let stand 15 minutes

to cool slightly. Stir in cheese. In a small saucepan, melt remaining 3 tablespoons butter. Stir in lemon peel, lemon juice, and basil; set aside. Rinse chicken; pat dry with paper towels. Sprinkle cavity with salt. Stuff cavity and neck lightly. Secure neck skin to back of chicken with skewers. Press wings over breast and tie with heavy string. Tie legs together; tie legs to tail. Insert spit rod under legs and through center of bird. Secure with holding fork. Test balance; attach to spit. Turn on motor. Grill over drip pan surrounded by medium-hot coals 1½ to 2 hours or until tender, basting often with lemon-butter mixture.

Spit Roasted Whole Chicken

Makes 4 servings

> 1 broiler-fryer chicken (2½ to 3 pounds)
> Salt
> Honey Glaze (recipe follows)

Sprinkle cavity of chicken with salt. Secure neck skin to back of chicken with skewers. Press wings over breast and tie with heavy string. Tie legs together; tie legs to tail. Insert spit rod under legs and through center of bird. Secure with holding forks. Test balance; attach to spit. Turn on motor. Grill over drip pan surrounded by medium-hot coals 1½ to 2 hours or until tender, basting with Honey Glaze the last 20 minutes of cooking time.

Honey Glaze

Makes about 1 cup

> ½ cup honey
> ½ cup soy sauce
> 2 cloves garlic, minced
> 3 tablespoons catsup

In a small bowl, combine all ingredients; blend well.

Stuffed Turkey

Makes 10 to 12 servings

- 1 frozen turkey (8 to 15 pounds), thawed
- 8 ounces bulk pork sausage
- 1 cup chopped celery
- 1 cup chopped onions
- 8 ounces mushrooms, sliced
- 1 bag (16 ounces) seasoned stuffing mix
- 1 loaf white *or* whole wheat bread, torn into pieces and dried
  Boiling water
- 3 eggs, lightly beaten
  Melted butter

Remove neck and giblets. Rinse turkey; pat dry. In a skillet, brown sausage. Push sausage to side of pan. Add celery, onions, and mushrooms. Sauté until tender-crisp; drain fat; set aside. In a large bowl, combine stuffing mix and dried bread. Cut butter into pieces; add to bread. Pour enough boiling water over bread to moisten as desired. Add sausage and vegetables; blend well. Add eggs; blend well. Fill neck and body cavity lightly with stuffing. Truss. (For best results, insert a meat thermometer between the leg and thigh without touching bone.) Place turkey on grill over drip pan. Grill over medium coals 13 minutes per pound with the lid on and dampers adjusted according to manufacturer's instructions. Add coals to each side of drip pan every hour. Baste often with melted butter during the last 1½ hours cooking time. Let stand 15 minutes before carving.

Lemon Duckling

Makes 2 servings

- 1 frozen duckling (about 5 pounds), thawed
- 1 can (6 ounces) frozen lemon concentrate, thawed
  Grated peel from ½ lemon
- 1 tablespoon cider vinegar

Pierce duck with a sharp fork in several places. Place on a rack in a roasting pan. Bake at 400° F. 1 hour. In a small bowl, combine lemonade concentrate, lemon peel, and vinegar; blend well. Secure neck skin to back of duckling with skewers. Press wings over breast and tie with heavy string. Tie legs together; tie legs to tail. Insert spit rod under legs and through center of bird. Secure with holding forks. Test balance; attach to spit. Turn on motor. Grill over drip pans surrounded by medium-hot coals for 30 minutes or until tender, basting often with lemon marinade.

Orange Smoked Turkey

Makes 10 to 12 servings

- 1 thawed frozen turkey (8 to 10 pounds), giblets and neck removed from cavity and rinsed
- 2 oranges, cut in halves
- 1 teaspoon poultry seasoning
- 1 small onion, quartered
- 1 rib celery, cut in pieces

Prepare grill for smoking. (See page 29.) Rub turkey with 2 of the orange halves. Rub poultry seasoning on outside and inside of turkey. Place oranges, onion, and celery in cavity. Secure neck skin to back of turkey with skewers. Press wings over breast and tie with heavy string. Tie legs together; tie legs to tail. (For best results, insert a meat thermometer between leg and thigh without touching bone.) Place a pan of water under center of grill. Place turkey about 6 inches above low coals and smoking chips and over pan of water. Smoke 7 to 8 hours, adding water to pan and smoking chips and hot coals to firebed every hour. Let stand 20 minutes before carving.

Tex-Mex Chicken

Makes 4 servings

- 1 broiler-fryer chicken (2½ to 3 pounds), halved
- 1 lemon, cut in half
- 6 cloves garlic, minced
- 1 tablespoon cayenne pepper
- 2 tablespoons paprika
  Salt

Rub chicken with lemon halves. Sprinkle with garlic, cayenne, paprika, and salt to taste; rub into skin. Refrigerate overnight. Grill over medium-hot coals 45 minutes or until tender, turning often.

Minted Chicken

Makes 6 servings

- ½ cup honey
- ¼ cup vegetable oil
- 2 tablespoons snipped mint leaves *or* mint flakes
  Salt
- 2 pounds chicken thighs

In a small bowl, combine honey, oil, mint, and salt to taste; blend well. Grill thighs over low coals about 15 minutes, turning once. Baste with honey glaze and grill 20 minutes, turning and basting often.

Fish and Shellfish

Soy Barbecued Shrimp

Makes 4 servings

- 2 pounds raw fresh *or* thawed frozen shrimp
- 2 cloves garlic, mashed
- ½ teaspoon salt
- ½ cup soy sauce
- ½ cup lemon *or* lime juice
- 3 tablespoons finely chopped parsley
- 2 teaspoons onion flakes
- ½ teaspoon black pepper

Shell and devein shrimp, leaving tails intact. Arrange shrimp in a shallow 1½-quart baking dish. In a small bowl, combine garlic and salt. Stir in remaining ingredients. Pour marinade over shrimp. Refrigerate 1 hour. Drain marinade from shrimp; reserve marinade. Thread shrimp on skewers. Place skewers in a well-greased hinged wire grill 4 inches above medium-hot coals. Grill 3 minutes, basting with marinade. Turn. Grill 5 minutes, basting several times with marinade. Serve remaining marinade as a dip.

Shrimp Scampi

Makes 6 servings

- ¾ cup butter *or* margarine
- 2 cloves garlic, minced
- ½ teaspoon crushed leaf tarragon
- ½ teaspoon crushed leaf rosemary
- ½ teaspoon crushed leaf thyme
- 3 tablespoons lemon juice
- 2 pounds raw fresh *or* thawed frozen uncooked large shrimp (15 to 20 per pound), shelled and deveined
- Salt and pepper
- 1 loaf French bread, wrapped in aluminum foil

In a small saucepan, combine butter, garlic, tarragon, rosemary, and thyme. Melt over low heat; let stand 3 to 4 minutes to blend flavors. Add lemon juice. Tear off six 12-inch pieces of heavy-duty aluminum foil. Arrange 4 or 5 shrimp on each piece of foil. Pour garlic-butter mixture over shrimp. Season each serving with salt and pepper to taste. Bring foil up and over shrimp; seal tightly. Grill over medium-hot coals 10 to 20 minutes or until shrimp is tender. Place French bread on grill the last 5 minutes of cooking time. Cook 5 minutes, turning once. Serve with shrimp.

Bacon and Onion Grilled Fish

Makes 4 servings

- 2 pounds pan-dressed fresh *or* thawed frozen fish
- ¾ cup margarine *or* butter, melted
- 1 envelope (1½ ounces) onion soup mix
- ¼ teaspoon black pepper
- ⅓ pound sliced bacon

Rinse and pat fish dry. In a small bowl, combine margarine, soup mix, and pepper; blend well. Brush fish inside and outside with butter mixture. Wrap a bacon slice around each fish. Place fish in a well-greased hinged wire grill about 5 inches above medium-hot coals. Grill 10 to 15 minutes. Baste with butter mixture; turn. Grill 10 to 15 minutes or until fish flakes easily when tested with a fork.

Grilled Fish with Orange Barbecue Sauce

Makes 4 servings

- 1½ pounds fresh *or* thawed frozen fish fillets
- ¾ teaspoon salt
- ¼ teaspoon black pepper
- Orange Barbecue Sauce (recipe follows)
- Orange slices, optional

Skin fillets and cut in serving portions. Sprinkle on salt and pepper. Brush both sides with Orange Barbecue Sauce. Place fillets in a well-greased hinged wire grill about 4 inches above medium-hot coals. Grill 5 to 8 minutes; baste with sauce. Turn and grill 5 to 8 minutes or until fish flakes easily when tested with a fork. Garnish with orange slices, if desired.

Orange Barbecue Sauce

Makes about 1 cup

- ½ cup orange juice
- ⅓ cup catsup
- 3 tablespoons brown sugar
- 2 tablespoons lemon juice
- 1 tablespoon instant minced onion
- 1 tablespoon soy sauce
- ¼ teaspoon salt

In a small saucepan, combine all ingredients. Cook over low heat until heated through, stirring often.

Fish/Shellfish

Oyster Supreme

Makes 4 servings

    24 shell oysters
 1/3 cup butter or margarine, melted
    3 tablespoons chopped onion
    2 tablespoons chopped drained pimiento
    1 tablespoon chopped parsley
  1/4 teaspoon salt
  1/4 teaspoon hot pepper sauce
  1/4 teaspoon Worcestershire sauce
  1/4 teaspoon dry mustard

Shuck and drain oysters. Place oysters on deep half of shells. In a skillet, melt butter. Add onion; sauté until onion is tender but not brown. Add remaining ingredients. Spoon sauce over oysters. Place oysters on grill over medium-hot coals. Grill 20 to 25 minutes or until edges begin to curl.

Zesty Shrimp

Makes 4 servings

 1½ pounds raw jumbo fresh or thawed frozen shrimp
    1 bottle (8 ounces) zesty Italian dressing
  1/2 teaspoon salt

Peel and devein shrimp. In a 2-quart bowl, combine Italian dressing and salt; blend well. Add shrimp; stir to coat with dressing. Refrigerate 30 minutes, stirring occasionally. Drain shrimp from dressing; reserve dressing. Place shrimp in a well-greased, hinged wire grill 4 inches above medium-hot coals. Grill 4 to 6 minutes; baste with dressing. Turn and grill 6 to 8 minutes or until shrimp are tender.

Backyard Scallops

Makes 4 servings

    1 pound fresh or thawed frozen bay scallops
  1/4 cup vegetable oil
  1/4 cup lemon juice
    1 teaspoon salt
  1/8 teaspoon hickory liquid smoke
    1 package (8 ounces) sliced bacon, partially cooked
      and cut in thirds
  1/2 cup sesame seed

Rinse scallops in cold water to remove any shell. In a 2-quart bowl, combine oil, lemon juice, salt, and liquid smoke. Add scallops; toss lightly to coat. Cover and refrigerate 30 minutes, stirring occasionally. Remove scallops from marinade. Wrap a bacon piece around each scallop; fasten with a wooden pick. Roll scallops in sesame seed. Place in a well-greased hinged wire grill, about 4 inches above medium-hot coals. Grill 2 to 4 minutes or until sesame seed browns. Turn and grill 2 to 4 minutes or until tender.

Oyster Kebabs

Makes 4 servings

 1/3 cup olive or vegetable oil
    2 tablespoons dry vermouth
    1 teaspoon chopped parsley
  1/4 teaspoon crushed leaf marjoram
  1/4 teaspoon crushed leaf thyme
  1/8 teaspoon black pepper
  1/8 teaspoon garlic salt
    1 can (15½ ounces) select oysters, rinsed and drained
    1 large green pepper, cut in 1-inch pieces
  1/2 pound fresh mushrooms
   10 slices bacon, cut in thirds

In a small bowl, combine oil, vermouth, parsley, and herbs and spices; blend well. Add oysters, green pepper, and mushrooms to marinade. Cover and refrigerate 1 hour. Drain marinade from oysters; reserve marinade. Wrap a piece of bacon around each oyster. Thread oysters and vegetables on four 12-inch skewers. Place skewers in a well-greased hinged wire grill 4 inches above medium-hot coals. Grill 5 to 7 minutes; baste with sauce. Turn and grill until bacon is crisp.

Backyard Patio Fish Supreme

Makes 4 servings

 1½ pounds fresh or thawed frozen thick fish fillets
  1/2 cup vegetable oil
  1/2 cup sesame seed
 1/3 cup brandy
 1/3 cup lemon juice
    3 tablespoons soy sauce
    1 teaspoon salt
    1 large clove garlic, crushed

Cut fish in serving portions. Place fish in a single layer in a 12 x 8-inch baking pan. In a small bowl, combine remaining ingredients. Pour marinade over fish. Cover and refrigerate 30 minutes, turning once. Drain marinade from fish; reserve marinade. Place fish in a well-greased hinged wire grill about 4 inches above medium-hot coals. Grill 8 minutes; baste with marinade. Turn and grill 7 to 10 minutes or until fish flakes easily when tested with a fork.

Smoking Fish

Smoked fish, meat, and poultry can be successfully produced in hooded or covered electric, gas or charcoal grills. Cooking times for smoke cooking will vary according to the type of equipment being used, the heat of the fire, and the distance the fish is from the heat source. Temperatures should be adjusted according to the recipe used, and for best results, use an oven thermometer if using a charcoal grill.

The best choices for smoking are fat fish, such as mullet, mackerel, blue fish, or salmon. Good results can also be obtained using lean fish, such as trout, catfish, and carp if they are basted frequently with cooking oil during the smoking process. Fat fish should be basted only near the end of cooking time.

To smoke fish, soak 1 pound of hardwood chips (hickory, apple, oak or cherry) in 2 quarts of water for several hours or overnight. Spread about one-third of the chips over coals or ceramic briquets. Add the remaining chips as needed while the fish is being smoked.

For stronger flavor, low temperatures (150° to 175° F.) are required. Good results can be obtained, however, in temperatures up to 300° F., which will reduce cooking time.

The same procedure for smoking is used regardless of the type of grill being used.

Smoked fish will keep 3 days if wrapped loosely and refrigerated.

To freeze smoked fish, wrap loosely and refrigerate until chilled. Rewrap in moisture-vapor-proof freezer wrap and place in the freezer. Smoked fish can be frozen up to 3 months. To use, remove freezer paper, wrap in aluminum foil, and heat 20 to 30 minutes in a 300° F. oven.

Seafood Smoking Chart

Size 'n' shape	How much to serve 4	How long to marinate in brine*	Cook at one of these temperatures	How long
Butterfly fillets (including bone, 1 pound each)	4 pounds	30 minutes	150°-175°F. 200°F. 250°F.	1 hr. + 30 min. 45 min. 30 min.
Fillets or steaks (½ inch thick)	1½ pounds	30 minutes	150°-175°F. 200°F. 250°F.	1 hr. 30 min. 20 min.
Fillets or steaks (¾ inch thick)	1½ pounds	45 minutes	150°-175°F. 200°F. 250°F.	1 hr. + 30 min. 30-45 min. 30 min.
Fillets or steaks (1 inch thick)	1½ pounds	45 minutes	150°-175°F. 200°F. 250°F.	1 hr. + 45 min. 30-45 min. 30 min.
Fillets or steaks (1½ inches thick)	1½ pounds	1 hour	150°-175°F. 200°F. 250°F.	2 hours 1 hr. + 15 min. 45-50 min.
Pan-dressed	2½ pounds	30 minutes	150°-175°F. 200°F. 250°F.	2 hours 1 hr. + 15 min. 45-50 min.

*To Brine Fish: Thaw fish if frozen. Combine 1 gallon cold water and 1 cup salt; stir until dissolved. Marinate fish in brine in refrigerator for 30 minutes before smoking. Rinse fish thoroughly in cold water and dry carefully after brining.

Plain Delicious Smoked Fish

Makes 6 servings

- 4 pounds fresh *or* thawed frozen fish fillets
- 1 cup salt
- 1 gallon water
- 1 box (3 ounces) crab boil (in pouch)
  Vegetable oil

Prepare the grill for smoking. (See page 29.) Clean and rinse fish fillets in cold water. In a 2-gallon bowl, combine salt and 1 gallon water. Add pouch of crab boil. Add fish; refrigerate 30 minutes, stirring occasionally. Remove fish from brine; rinse well and pat dry. Place fish fillets, skin side down, on a well-greased grill 4 to 6 inches above smoking chips in smoke oven. Close hood on grill; open vent slightly to keep smoke and air circulating. Smoke fish about 1 hour at 150° to 175° F. or 30 to 45 minutes at 200° F. Baste fish with vegetable oil near end of cooking time. Fish is done when the cut surface is golden brown and flesh flakes easily when tested with a fork.

Smokehouse Oysters

Makes 4 servings

- 12 shell oysters, shucked and drained
- ⅛ teaspoon salt
- ⅛ teaspoon black pepper
- ¼ cup butter *or* margarine, softened
- 2 tablespoons chopped green onion
- 2 tablespoons chopped parsley
- ¼ cup cornflake crumbs
- ¼ cup grated Parmesan cheese
  Rock salt
  Chopped parsley

Prepare the grill for smoking. (See page 29.) Place oysters on deep half of shell. Sprinkle on salt and pepper. In a small bowl, combine butter, onion, and parsley; blend well. Dot oysters with butter mixture. In a small bowl, combine cornflake crumbs and cheese; blend well. Sprinkle over oysters. In a shallow 9 x 11-inch aluminum foil pan, place a layer of rock salt 1 inch deep. Place oyster shells on top of the rock salt. Place pan on grill about 4 inches above hot coals and smoking chips in smoke oven. Smoke 15 to 20 minutes or until tops are brown and edges of oysters curl. Garnish with chopped parsley.

Note: Rock salt is used to hold shells upright and to keep the oysters hot.

Smoked Fish with Ginger Sauce

Makes 4 servings

- Ginger Sauce (recipe follows)
- 1½ pounds fresh *or* thawed frozen fish fillets
- ¾ teaspoon salt
- ¼ teaspoon black pepper

Prepare the grill for smoking. (See page 29.) Prepare Ginger Sauce; set aside. Cut fish fillets into serving portions. Season with salt and pepper. Brush both sides with Ginger Sauce. Place fillets on a well-greased grill about 4 inches above medium-hot coals and smoking chips in smoke oven. Smoke 10 to 15 minutes; baste with sauce. Smoke 10 to 15 minutes or until fish flakes easily when tested with a fork.

Ginger Sauce

Makes about 1 cup

- ½ cup catsup
- ¼ cup chicken broth
- 2 tablespoons soy sauce
- 1 tablespoon honey
- 2 teaspoons grated fresh gingerroot

In a small bowl, combine all ingredients; blend well.

Smoked Scallop Kebabs

Makes 4 servings

- ½ pound fresh *or* thawed frozen bay *or* calico scallops
- 12 lime slices
- 4 slices Canadian bacon, cut in half
- ¼ cup lime juice
- ¼ cup butter *or* margarine, melted
- ¼ cup grated Parmesan cheese
- ½ teaspoon salt
- ¼ cup chopped parsley

Prepare the grill for smoking. (See page 29.) Rinse scallops in cold water to remove any shell. Alternately thread scallops, lime slices, and Canadian bacon on four 10-inch skewers. In a small bowl, combine lime juice and butter; blend well. Baste scallops with marinade. In a small bowl, combine cheese, salt, and parsley; blend well. Sprinkle on scallops. Place skewers on a well greased grill about 4 inches above medium-hot coals and smoking chips in smoke oven. Smoke 4 to 6 minutes. Turn and smoke 4 to 6 minutes or until scallops are tender.

Packet Meals

Foods that are irregular in shape or contain a lot of moisture are made easily and deliciously when wrapped in individual packets and grilled. Following are instructions for two methods of wrapping foil packets. Use whichever method you feel is best for your recipe.

Drugstore Wrap

Place the food in the center of an oblong piece of heavy-duty aluminum foil, being certain that the foil is large enough to fold at the top and sides. (Fig. A)

A

Bring two sides together above the food, then fold down loosely in a series of locked folds allowing for heat circulation and expansion. (Fig. B)

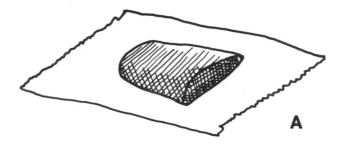

B

Fold the short ends up and over again and crimp edges to seal. The ends can be rolled or twisted to close the packet or the fold can be made on the side of the packet. Foods tend to cook more evenly with the thick fold at the side. (Fig. C)

C

Bundle Wrap

Tear off a piece of heavy-duty aluminum foil large enough to allow adequate folding and wrapping. Place food in the center of the foil. (Fig. A)

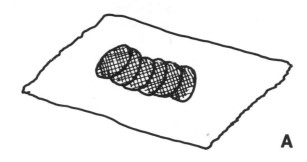

A

Bring four corners up and into the center. (Fig. B)

B

Fold the openings together loosely to allow for heat circulation and expansion. (Fig. C)

C

Seal by folding over ends and pressing to the package (Fig. D)

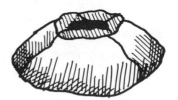

D

Parmesan Potatoes

Makes 4 servings

    4 large baking potatoes
    Onion salt
    Celery salt
    Black pepper
    ½ cup grated Parmesan cheese
    ½ cup butter *or* margarine

Scrub potatoes; do not peel. Cut lengthwise into ¼-inch-thick slices. Spread on a 20-inch length of heavy-duty aluminum foil. Sprinkle on onion and celery salts and pepper. Sprinkle on Parmesan cheese. Arrange potato slices in center of foil. Dot with butter. Bring foil up and over potatoes; seal tightly. Grill over medium-hot coals 30 to 45 minutes or until tender, turning several times.

Chutney Shrimp

Makes 4 servings

    1 pound raw fresh *or* thawed frozen shrimp,
        peeled and deveined
    1 medium onion, sliced
    1 medium green pepper, cut in rings
    2 medium carrots, cut in 3-inch sticks
    1 jar (9 ounces) chutney
        Chopped parsley

Tear off 4 large pieces of heavy-duty aluminum foil; grease lightly. Divide shrimp, onion, green pepper, and carrots among pieces of foil. Spoon 1 tablespoon chutney over shrimp. Bring foil up and over shrimp; seal tightly. Grill about 4 inches above medium-hot coals 10 to 15 minutes or until shrimp is tender. Heat remaining chutney and serve with shrimp. Garnish with parsley.

Chicken Packets

Makes 4 servings

    1 broiler-fryer chicken (3 to 3½ pounds), quartered
    ¼ cup butter *or* margarine
    1 envelope (1½ ounces) onion soup mix
    1 teaspoon paprika
    1 can (4 ounces) mushroom stems and pieces, drained
    ½ cup half-and-half

Rinse chicken, pat dry, and remove any small protruding bones. Tear off 4 pieces of heavy-duty aluminum foil. On each piece of foil, place 1 teaspoon butter, 1 tablespoon soup mix, and ½ teaspoon paprika. Place a chicken quarter in center of foil. Sprinkle on remaining soup mix and butter. Divide mushrooms among packets. Spoon 2 tablespoons half-and-half over each chicken packet. Bring foil up and over chicken; seal tightly. Grill over medium-hot coals about 45 minutes or until tender, turning chicken packets every 10 minutes.

Garden Pot Roast

Makes 6 to 8 servings

    1 package (½ ounce) Italian salad dressing mix
    ¼ cup flour
    1 teaspoon salt
    ½ teaspoon paprika
    ⅛ teaspoon black pepper
    1 beef blade roast (3 to 4 pounds)
    2 cups thinly sliced carrots
    2 cups sliced zucchini (¾-inch slices)

In a small bowl, combine salad dressing mix, flour, salt, paprika, and pepper; blend well. Place roast in the center of a double thickness piece of heavy-duty aluminum foil. Coat both sides of roast with flour mixture. Bring foil up and over meat; seal tightly. Grill over medium-hot coals 1½ hours, turning after 1 hour. Remove foil packet from grill; open carefully. Place carrots and zucchini on roast. Reseal packet. Grill over medium-hot coals about 30 minutes or until vegetables and meat are tender. Do not turn packet.

Stuffed Chicken Breasts

Makes 6 servings

    1 package (10 ounces) frozen chopped spinach,
        thawed and drained
    1 cup seasoned stuffing mix
    1 can (7½ ounces) ready-to-serve cream of
        mushroom soup
    ¾ cup grated Cheddar cheese
    2 teaspoons minced onion
    6 whole chicken breasts, skinned, boned,
        and split
        Salt
        Paprika

Tear off 6 pieces of heavy-duty aluminum foil. In a medium bowl, combine spinach, stuffing mix, soup, cheese, and onion; blend well. Place about ½ cup spinach mixture in center of each piece of foil. Place chicken breast on spinach mixture; fold sides under. Season with salt and paprika to taste. Bring foil up and over chicken; seal tightly. Grill over medium-hot coals about 40 minutes or until chicken is tender, turning once.

Packet Meals

Fish Banquet

Makes 2 servings

- 1 fish (1 pound)
- 2 slices bacon
- 2 potatoes, peeled and quartered
- 1 onion, sliced
- Salt and pepper

Tear off a large double thickness of heavy-duty aluminum foil. Place 1 slice bacon on foil. Place fish on top of bacon. Top with remaining bacon slice. Arrange potatoes and onion on top of fish. Season with salt and pepper to taste. Bring foil up and over fish; seal tightly. Grill over indirect heat 15 to 20 minutes on each side or until fish flakes easily with a fork. Serve directly from packet.

Grilled Fish in a Packet

- 1 fish, scaled and cleaned, whole or cut in steaks
- Vegetable oil or melted butter
- Salt and pepper
- Lemon juice
- 2 tablespoons chopped tomato
- Lemon slices

Tear off a large sheet of heavy-duty aluminum foil. Place fish on foil. Brush fish with oil. Season with salt and pepper, and lemon juice to taste. Top with chopped tomato. Garnish with lemon slices. Bring foil up and over fish; seal tightly. Grill over medium-hot coals 10 minutes on each side for a 1 to 1½-pound fish; 20 minutes per side for 4 to 5-pound fish. Fish is done when it flakes easily with a fork.

Fresh Vegetable Packets

Makes 4 servings

- 2 medium tomatoes, sliced ½ inch thick
- 2 medium onions, sliced
- 2 medium green peppers, cut in rings
- 12 mushrooms, halved
- Salt and pepper
- 4 teaspoons butter

Tear off 4 large pieces of heavy-duty aluminum foil. Divide tomatoes, onions, and green peppers among foil, overlapping pieces in rows. Top with mushrooms. Season with salt and pepper to taste. Dot each with 1 teaspoon butter. Bring foil up and over vegetables; seal tightly. Grill over medium-hot coals 15 minutes.

Backyard Clambake

Makes 4 servings

- Seaweed, optional
- 12 steamer clams, scrubbed
- 1 fresh or thawed frozen lobster (about 1 pound), rinsed and split
- ½ small broiler-fryer chicken (about 1½ pounds), cut in serving pieces and sharp bones removed
- 1 ear corn, husked and quartered
- 1 small onion, quartered
- 1 potato, cut lengthwise in eighths
- Salt and pepper
- Melted butter

Tear off 4 large pieces of heavy-duty aluminum foil. Cover each with a piece of cheesecloth cut to fit. If you are using seaweed, place a handful on the cheesecloth. Top with clams, lobster, and chicken. Tuck in corn, onion, and potato wherever there is room. Season with salt and pepper to taste. (If you are not using seaweed, add ¼ cup water to each packet.) Tie cheesecloth up and over food. Bring foil up and over food; seal tightly. Grill over medium-hot coals 45 minutes to 1 hour or until chicken is tender. Open a packet after 35 minutes to test chicken for doneness. If it is not tender, close packet and return to grill. Serve with individual bowls of melted butter for dipping.

Beef and Vegetables Packet

Makes 6 servings

- 1 beef chuck steak (about 2 pounds), cut in 1-inch cubes
- 6 medium potatoes, peeled and diced
- 6 tablespoons chopped onion
- 6 carrots, peeled and sliced
- ½ cup chopped parsley
- 2 cans (10¾ ounces each) cream of mushroom soup, undiluted
- 6 tablespoons water
- Salt and pepper
- Hot pepper sauce

Tear off 6 large pieces of heavy-duty aluminum foil. Divide all ingredients into six portions and place on foil pieces. Add 1 tablespoon water to each portion. Season with salt and pepper to taste. Sprinkle on hot pepper sauce to taste. Bring foil up and over food; seal tightly. Grill over hot coals 1 hour or until beef is done and potatoes are tender.

Grilled Fish in a Packet   Oregano Dip, 54
French Fries in a Poke, 40   Canned Green Pea Soup
Broccoli and Cheese Casserole, 38

Breads and Sandwiches

Hard Rolls with Lemon Butter

Makes 12 servings

- ½ cup butter *or* margarine
- 2 tablespoons chopped parsley
- 1 tablespoon lemon juice
- 12 hard rolls, split

In a small bowl, combine butter, parsley, and lemon juice; blend well. Spread rolls with lemon butter. Wrap each roll in sheet of heavy-duty aluminum foil. Grill 10 to 15 minutes or until heated through, turning occasionally.

Herb Bread

Makes 12 servings

- 1 cup butter *or* margarine
- ¾ cup minced chives
- ¾ cup chopped parsley
- 2 tablespoons minced basil
- Garlic salt
- 1 loaf French bread

In a small bowl, combine butter, chives, parsley, basil, and garlic salt to taste; blend well. Slice bread diagonally about ¾ inch apart without cutting through bottom crust. Spread herb butter between slices and on top of bread. Wrap loaf in a sheet of heavy-duty aluminum foil. Grill about 15 minutes or until heated through, turning occasionally.

Blue Cheese and Herb Bread

Makes 12 servings

- 1 cup butter, softened
- 4 ounces crumbled blue cheese
- 2 teaspoons minced onion
- 1 teaspoon crushed leaf rosemary
- 1 teaspoon crushed leaf basil
- 2 tablespoons chopped parsley
- 1 loaf French bread

In a small bowl, combine all ingredients, except bread; blend well. Slice bread diagonally about ¾ inch apart without cutting through bottom crust. Spread herb and cheese mixture between slices and on top of bread. Wrap loaf in a sheet of heavy-duty aluminum foil. Grill about 15 minutes or until heated through, turning occasionally.

Quick Garlic Bread

Makes 12 servings

- ½ cup butter *or* margarine, softened
- 1 clove garlic, minced *or* ⅛ teaspoon garlic powder
- 1 loaf French bread

In a small bowl, combine butter and garlic; blend well. Slice bread diagonally about ¾ inch apart without cutting through bottom crust. Spread garlic butter between slices and on top of bread. Wrap loaf in a sheet of heavy-duty aluminum foil. Grill about 15 minutes or until heated through, turning occasionally.

French Bread with Cheese

Makes 12 to 14 servings

- ½ cup butter *or* margarine
- ½ cup grated Swiss cheese
- ¼ cup crumbled cooked bacon
- 1 tablespoon minced chives
- 2 teaspoons poppy seed
- 1 tablespoon prepared mustard
- ½ teaspoon grated lemon peel
- 1½ teaspoons lemon juice
- Dash pepper
- 1 loaf French bread

In a small bowl, combine all ingredients, except bread; blend well. Slice bread diagonally about ¾ inch apart without cutting through bottom crust. Spread cheese mixture between slices and on top of bread. Wrap loaf in a sheet of heavy-duty aluminum foil. Grill about 20 minutes or until heated through and cheese is melted, turning occasionally.

Onion Bread

Makes 12 servings

- 1 cup butter *or* margarine
- 1 tablespoon chopped parsley
- 1 envelope (1½ ounces) onion soup mix
- 2 loaves brown-and-serve French bread

In a small bowl, combine butter, parsley, and onion soup mix; blend well. Slice bread diagonally about ¾ inch apart without cutting through bottom crust. Spread onion butter between slices and on top of bread. Make an aluminum foil pan to fit each loaf. Place loaves on grill. Grill about 15 minutes or until hot and lightly browned.

Grilled Parmesan Toast

Makes 8 servings

- ½ cup butter *or* margarine, softened
- ¼ cup grated Parmesan cheese
- 2 tablespoons chopped parsley
- 1 loaf Italian bread

In a small bowl, combine butter, cheese, and parsley; blend well. Slice bread about 1½ inches apart; split lengthwise cutting through bottom crust. Spread cheese butter between slices. Toast about 5 minutes on each side or until golden brown.

Smoked Fish and Olive Sandwiches

Makes 4 servings

- 1 cup flaked smoked fish
- 1 tablespoon minced pimiento-stuffed green olives
- 1 cup grated sharp Cheddar cheese
- ⅓ cup mayonnaise *or* salad dressing
- ¼ teaspoon Worcestershire sauce
- ¼ teaspoon garlic salt
- ⅛ teaspoon black pepper
- 4 onion rolls, split
  Whole pimiento-stuffed green olives, optional

In a medium bowl, combine all ingredients, except onion rolls and whole olives. Place about ⅒ cup fish mixture on bottom half of each roll. Cover with top of roll. Wrap each sandwich in a piece of heavy-duty aluminum foil. Grill over medium-hot coals 10 to 15 minutes or until cheese melts. Garnish with olives on a wooden pick, if desired.

Hot Ham and Cheese Rolls

Makes 8 to 12 servings

- ½ pound boiled ham, cut in ½-inch pieces
- ½ pound processed sharp cheese, cut in ½-inch cubes
- ¼ cup chopped onion
- ½ cup pimiento-stuffed olives, sliced
- 2 hard-cooked eggs, coarsely chopped
- 2 tablespoons mayonnaise
- ½ cup tomato paste
- 8 to 12 frankfurter rolls, split

In a small bowl, combine ham, cheese, onion, olives, and eggs. Add mayonnaise and tomato paste; blend well. Divide among frankfurter rolls, spreading evenly. Wrap each sandwich in a piece of heavy-duty aluminum foil; twist ends tightly to seal. Grill over hot coals until heated through.

Taco Franks

Makes 8 servings

- ½ cup chili sauce
  Dash hot pepper sauce
- 1 teaspoon chili powder
- 8 frankfurter rolls, split
- 4 slices American cheese, cut in half
- 8 frankfurters
- 1 cup shredded lettuce
- 1 cup chopped tomatoes

In a small bowl, combine chili and hot pepper sauces, and chili powder; blend well. Spread each frankfurter roll with chili sauce mixture. Place a piece of cheese in each roll. Add frankfurters. Top with lettuce and tomatoes. Wrap each sandwich in a piece of heavy-duty aluminum foil. Grill over low heat 15 minutes or until frankfurters are hot and cheese is melted, turning occasionally.

Beef and Cheese Sandwiches

Makes 6 servings

- 1 pound lean ground beef
- 1 tablespoon minced onion
- ½ cup tomato sauce
- ½ cup catsup
- 2 tablespoons grated Parmesan cheese
- ½ teaspoon garlic powder
- ¼ teaspoon fennel seed
- ⅛ teaspoon ground oregano
- 6 Kaiser rolls, split
  Garlic Butter (recipe follows)
- 6 slices mozzarella cheese

In a large skillet, brown ground beef and onion, stirring to break up meat; drain fat. Stir in tomato sauce, catsup, Parmesan cheese, garlic powder, fennel seed, and oregano. Simmer 20 minutes, stirring occasionally. Spread rolls with Garlic Butter. Divide meat mixture among rolls. Top each with a slice of cheese. Wrap each sandwich in a piece of heavy-duty aluminum foil; twist ends tightly to seal. Grill over hot coals about 15 minutes or until cheese melts.

Garlic Butter

- 2 tablespoons butter, softened
- ¼ teaspoon garlic powder
- ½ teaspoon paprika

In a small bowl, combine all ingredients; blend well.

Vegetables and Rice

Broccoli and Cheese Casserole

Makes 4 to 6 servings

    6 tablespoons butter *or* margarine, divided
    ¼ cup minced onion
    2 tablespoons flour
    ½ cup water
    1 jar (8 ounces) processed cheese spread
    2 packages (10 ounces each) frozen chopped
      broccoli, thawed and drained
    3 eggs, well beaten
    ½ cup soft bread crumbs

In a skillet, melt 4 tablespoons butter. Add onion; sauté until onion is tender. Stir in flour; blend well. Gradually stir in water. Cook over low heat until thickened, stirring constantly. Blend in cheese. In an 11 x 7-inch aluminum foil pan, combine sauce, broccoli, and eggs; stir carefully to blend. Sprinkle crumbs over top. Dot with remaining 2 tablespoons butter. Grill over medium-hot coals about 30 minutes or until heated through.

Baked Bean Pot

Makes 6 to 8 servings

    1 pound dried beans (kidney, navy, lima, or
      combination)
    1 large onion, chopped
    1 green pepper, chopped
    2 tablespoons vegetable oil
    ¼ pound bacon, cut in pieces
    2 teaspoons salt
    1 can (16 ounces) tomatoes, undrained
    2 tablespoons brown sugar
    2 teaspoons prepared mustard
    ½ teaspoon hot pepper sauce
    ½ teaspoon Worcestershire sauce

Place beans in a large saucepan; cover with water. Bring to boiling; reduce heat. Cover and simmer about 1 hour. While beans are cooking, sauté onion and green pepper in oil 5 minutes or until tender. Add onion-green pepper mixture to beans along with remaining ingredients. Cover and simmer 1 hour, stirring occasionally. Add water, if necessary, to keep beans covered. Can be made ahead and reheated on the grill.

Baked Potatoes

Makes 4 servings

    4 medium baking potatoes
      Vegetable oil
      Salt and pepper
      Baked Potato Toppings

Scrub and rinse potatoes. Brush with oil. Place each potato on a piece of heavy-duty aluminum foil. Bring foil up and over potatoes; seal tightly. Grill over medium-hot coals 45 to 60 minutes, turning occasionally. Open foil. Slit each potato down center; fluff with a fork. Sprinkle on salt and pepper to taste. Top with your favorite topping.

Baked Potato Toppings

    Sour cream and chopped chives *or* parsley
    Cream cheese and chopped onion
    Chopped olives and sour cream
    Crumbled crisp bacon
    Sautéed sliced mushrooms
    Shredded Cheddar cheese
    Chopped green pepper
    Lemon-butter sauce
    Plain yogurt

Garden Casserole

Makes 6 to 8 servings

    3 small carrots, peeled and sliced
    ½ pound green beans, trimmed and sliced
    1 small yellow squash, sliced
    1 small zucchini, sliced
    ½ head cauliflower, broken into flowerets
    ¼ cup butter, divided
    1 clove garlic, minced
    1 cup chicken broth
    1 teaspoon salt
    ½ teaspoon white pepper

In a buttered 2-quart casserole, arrange all vegetables. In a small saucepan, melt 2 tablespoons butter. Add garlic; cook and stir until garlic is fragrant. Stir in broth, salt, and pepper. Pour broth over vegetables. Dot with remaining butter. Cover and bake at 350° F. 30 minutes or until all vegetables are tender.

Note: To cook on grill-top, use an aluminum pan and cover with foil.

Vegetables and Rice

Sherried Rice

Makes 4 to 6 servings

  1 tablespoon butter *or* margarine
  ½ cup sliced green onions
  1 can (4 ounces) mushroom stems and pieces, drained
  1 cup fresh *or* thawed frozen peas
  1 can (15 ounces) chicken broth
  ¾ cup dry sherry
  1 teaspoon salt
  ½ teaspoon white pepper
  1½ cups long-grain rice

Butter an 11 x 7-inch aluminum foil pan; set aside. In a saucepan, melt butter. Add onions; sauté until onions are tender. Add mushrooms, peas, broth, sherry, salt, and pepper. Stir in rice. Pour into prepared pan. Cover tightly with aluminum foil. Grill over medium-hot coals about 15 minutes or until rice is tender. Fluff with a fork and serve.

Grilled Onions

Makes 4 servings

  4 medium onions
    Salt and pepper
  4 tablespoons butter
  4 slices bacon, cut in half

Clean onions; remove a thin slice from top and bottom of each. Make a criss-cross cut from top ¾ of the way through onions. Sprinkle on salt and pepper to taste. Place 1 tablespoon butter in center of each onion. Lay 2 pieces bacon across top. Wrap each onion in a piece of heavy-duty aluminum foil. Grill over medium-hot coals 45 minutes or until onions are tender. To serve, place bacon under onion and pull sides down to form a flower.

French Fries in a Poke

Makes 4 servings

  1 bag (16 ounces) frozen French fries, partially thawed
    Salt and pepper

Tear off a large piece of heavy-duty aluminum foil. Place fries on foil. Season with salt and pepper to taste. Gather foil up and over French fries; seal tightly. Grill over medium-hot coals 15 minutes or until hot, shaking package occasionally.

Rice Pilaf

Makes 6 servings

  1½ cups long-grain rice
  3 cups water
  1 teaspoon salt
  ⅓ cup butter *or* margarine
  1 chicken bouillon cube
  ¼ teaspoon crushed leaf rosemary
  1 can (4 ounces) mushroom stems and pieces, drained

In a large saucepan, combine rice, water, salt, butter, bouillon, and rosemary. Bring to boiling; reduce heat. Cover and simmer 15 minutes. Let stand 5 minutes. Stir in mushrooms; let stand 2 to 3 minutes to heat through. Fluff with a fork and serve.

Parmesan Corn

Makes 8 servings

  ½ cup grated Parmesan cheese
  ½ cup butter *or* margarine, softened
  1 tablespoon chopped parsley
  ½ teaspoon salt
  8 ears corn, husked

In a small bowl, combine cheese, butter, parsley, and salt; blend well. Place each ear of corn on a piece of heavy-duty aluminum foil. Spread 1 tablespoon of butter mixture on each ear. Wrap corn tightly. Grill over medium-low coals 20 to 30 minutes or until corn is tender, turning once.

Crumb Topped Tomatoes

Makes 6 to 8 servings

  ½ cup soft bread crumbs
  2 tablespoons grated Parmesan cheese
    Dash salt
  ⅛ teaspoon black pepper
  6 medium tomatoes, halved
  2 tablespoons butter, melted

In a small bowl, combine bread crumbs, cheese, salt, and pepper; blend well. Top each tomato half with a spoonful of crumb mixture. Drizzle melted butter over each. Place each tomato, cut side up, on a piece of heavy-duty aluminum foil. Grill over medium-low coals 10 minutes or until heated through.

Salads and Relishes

Garden Tomato and Avocado Salad

Makes 4 servings

> Herbed French Dressing (recipe follows)
> ½ head lettuce *or* 1 bunch escarole
> Lemon juice
> 2 ripe avocados, peeled and sliced
> 4 large tomatoes, peeled and cut in wedges

Prepare Herbed French Dressing; chill. Wash, drain, and chill lettuce or escarole. Sprinkle lemon juice on avocados to keep from turning brown. Refrigerate about 1 hour. Arrange greens, tomatoes, and avocados in a salad bowl. Drizzle dressing over salad. Separate with a fork to coat with dressing but do not toss.

Herbed French Dressing

Makes about 1 cup

> ¾ cup olive *or* vegetable oil
> ¼ cup lemon juice
> 2 tablespoons minced chives
> 1 tablespoon minced fresh tarragon *or* 1 teaspoon crushed leaf tarragon
> 1 tablespoon minced dillweed *or* 1 teaspoon dried dillweed
> 2 teaspoons salt
> Dash pepper

In a small bowl, combine all ingredients; blend well. Refrigerate at least 30 minutes. Mix with a fork before using.

Quick Fruit Salad

Makes 8 to 10 servings

> 1 cantaloupe, cut in chunks
> 1 small jar (10 ounces) maraschino cherries, drained and halved
> 1 cup pineapple chunks, drained
> 1 cup mandarin orange segments, drained
> 1 banana, sliced
> 1 can (21 ounces) peach pie filling

In a medium bowl, combine all fruit. Stir in peach pie filling; blend well. Chill at least 1 hour before serving.

Note: Proportions of fruit can be varied without adding additional pie filling.

Macaroni Fruit Salad with Orange Dressing

Makes 6 to 8 servings

> 1 package (7 ounces) elbow macaroni, cooked according to package directions and drained
> ½ cup wheat germ
> 1 can (13¼ ounces) pineapple tidbits, drained; reserve juice
> 1 cup cantaloupe balls
> 1 can (4 ounces) mandarin orange segments, drained
> 1 cup seedless grape halves
> 1 carton (8 ounces) mandarin-orange-flavored yogurt
> 2 tablespoons honey
> Salad greens, optional

In a large bowl, place macaroni. Reserve 2 tablespoons wheat germ. Sprinkle remaining wheat germ over macaroni; blend well. Add pineapple, cantaloupe, oranges, and grapes; toss lightly to blend. In a small bowl, combine 2 tablespoons of the reserved pineapple juice, yogurt, and honey; blend well. Pour yogurt dressing over fruit and macaroni; blend well. Sprinkle reserved wheat germ over top of salad. Refrigerate until chilled, about 2 hours. Serve on crisp salad greens, if desired.

Summer Fruit Basket

Makes 8 to 10 servings

> ½ watermelon (slice lengthwise)
> 1 cantaloupe
> 1 quart strawberries
> 1 quart blueberries
> 1 quart cherries
> 1 fresh pineapple *or* 1 can (16 ounces) pineapple chunks, drained
> 3 limes, cut in wedges, optional
> Mint sprigs, optional

Use a melon scoop to make balls from watermelon and cantaloupe. Refrigerate melons while preparing basket. Hollow out watermelon shell. Use a sharp knife to make a scalloped or sawtooth edge on the watermelon. Combine melon balls, strawberries, blueberries, cherries, and pineapple in watermelon basket. Garnish with lime wedges and mint sprigs, if desired. Chill well before serving.

Note: Any fresh fruit can be substituted if some of those listed are not available.

Fire and Ice Tomatoes

Makes 6 to 8 servings

    Mustard Ring Mold (recipe follows)
    6 large tomatoes, thickly sliced
    ¼ cup minced onion
    2 teaspoons crushed leaf basil
    2 teaspoons salt, divided
    ¼ cup wine vinegar
    ¾ cup olive or vegetable oil
    1 clove garlic, minced
    1 teaspoon Worcestershire sauce
    ½ teaspoon black pepper
    ½ teaspoon sugar

Prepare Mustard Ring Mold. Line the bottom of a large serving bowl with tomato slices. In a separate bowl, combine onion, basil, and 1 teaspoon of the salt. Sprinkle some of the onion mixture over tomatoes in bowl. Layer remaining tomato slices, sprinkling onion mixture over each layer. In a stoppered jar or cruet, combine wine vinegar, olive oil, garlic, Worcestershire sauce, remaining 1 teaspoon salt, pepper, and sugar; shake to blend well. Pour dressing over tomatoes. Cover and refrigerate until well chilled. To serve, carefully tip bowl to drain excess liquid or transfer to Mustard Ring Mold with a slotted spoon.

Mustard Ring Mold

    1 envelope (¼ ounce) unflavored gelatin
    1½ cups cole slaw salad dressing
    ⅓ cup dry mustard
    2 cups whipping cream, whipped

Place gelatin in the top of a double boiler over slowly boiling water. Slowly stir in salad dressing; blend well. Stir in dry mustard. Cook until mixture is hot and gelatin is dissolved. Remove from heat; cool slightly Use a rubber spatula to gently fold the mustard mixture into the whipped cream. Rinse a 6-cup ring mold with cold water. Shake out excess water. Immediately pour mustard mixture into ring mold. Refrigerate 3 to 4 hours.

Texas Cole Slaw

Makes 8 servings

    1 medium head cabbage, cored and shredded
    1 large green pepper, thinly sliced
    1 large onion, thinly sliced
    ½ cup sugar
    1 cup cider vinegar
    1 tablespoon sugar
    1½ teaspoons celery seed   1 tablespoon dry mustard
                                       1 cup vegetable oil

In a large bowl, combine cabbage, green pepper, and onion. Sprinkle ½ cup sugar over top; toss lightly; set aside. In a medium saucepan, combine vinegar, 1 tablespoon sugar, celery seed, and mustard; bring to boiling, stirring constantly. Remove from heat. Stir in oil. Return to heat; bring to boiling. Pour hot mixture over cabbage mixture; toss lightly. Cover and refrigerate 8 hours or overnight. Before transporting or serving, drain slaw well in a colander.

Seven Layer Salad

Makes 6 to 8 servings

    1 head lettuce, torn into bite-size pieces
    1 cup chopped celery
    ½ cup chopped green onions
    1 cup diced green pepper
    1 package (10 ounces) frozen peas, cooked
      and drained
    4 hard-cooked eggs, sliced, optional
    2 tablespoons sugar
    2 cups mayonnaise
    ½ pound sliced bacon, cooked, drained, and crumbled
    4 ounces Cheddar cheese, shredded

In a large salad bowl, place lettuce. Layer celery, onions, green pepper, peas, and eggs over lettuce. Spread mayonnaise over top. Sprinkle sugar over mayonnaise. Sprinkle on bacon and cheese. Refrigerate until ready to serve.

Deluxe Potato Salad

Makes 6 to 8 servings

    8 medium potatoes or 12 new potatoes
    1 can (10½ ounces) chicken broth
    1 large red onion, minced
    12 cherry tomatoes
    1 can (4 ounces) artichoke hearts, drained
      and sliced
    4 hard-cooked eggs, diced
    Chopped parsley
    Salt and pepper
    1 cup mayonnaise or salad dressing

Boil the potatoes in their skins until tender, about 25 minutes; drain and set aside until cool. Peel and slice potatoes; place in a bowl. Pour chicken broth over potatoes; let stand for 1 hour. In a salad bowl, combine onion, tomatoes, artichoke hearts, and eggs. Sprinkle on parsley, and salt and pepper to taste. Just before serving, drain potatoes and add to vegetables; toss lightly. Stir in mayonnaise. If transporting, keep potato salad well chilled.

Salads

Calico Bean Salad

Makes 6 servings

 2 cups cut green beans, drained
 2 cups cut waxed beans, drained
 2 cups kidney beans, drained
 1 can (16 ounces) garbanzo beans, drained
 ½ large green pepper, sliced
 ½ large onion, sliced
 ¾ cup sugar
 ⅔ cup vinegar
 ⅓ cup vegetable oil
   Salt

In a large bowl, combine all the beans, green pepper, and onion; toss lightly to mix. In a small bowl, combine sugar, vinegar, oil, and salt to taste; blend well. Pour dressing over salad; toss lightly. Chill well, stirring occasionally.

Shrimp Macaroni Salad

Makes 4 to 6 servings

 1 box (7 ounces) ring macaroni, cooked according
   to package directions and drained
 1 cup pitted black olives, sliced
 1 can (6½ ounces) broken shrimp, drained
 6 hard-cooked eggs, chopped
 2 ribs celery, diced
 2 green onions, diced
 2 ounces mild Cheddar cheese, cubed
 ½ teaspoon onion salt
 1 cup mayonnaise *or* salad dressing

In a large bowl, combine macaroni, olives, shrimp, eggs, celery, onions, and cheese; toss lightly. Stir onion salt into mayonnaise; blend into macaroni mixture. Cover and refrigerate until chilled.

Crunchy Chicken Salad

Makes 4 servings

 1 cup diced cooked chicken
 1 cup diced celery
 1 cup shredded raw carrots
 ¼ cup minced onion
 1 tablespoon half-and-half *or* milk
 ½ cup mayonnaise *or* salad dressing
 1 tablespoon pickle relish
 1 can (2 ounces) shoestring potatoes

In a medium bowl, combine chicken, celery, carrots, and onion; toss lightly. In a separate small bowl, stir half-and-half into mayonnaise. Stir in relish. Add dressing to vegetables; blend well. Top with shoestring potatoes and serve.

German Potato Salad

Makes 6 to 8 servings

 10 medium potatoes
  1 pound sliced bacon, crisp-cooked, drained, and
    crumbled; reserve 2 tablespoons drippings
  1 tablespoon flour
  ¾ cup water
  ¼ cup vinegar
  ¼ cup sugar
  1 teaspoon salt
  1 small onion, minced
 1½ cups diced celery

Boil the potatoes in their skins until tender, about 25 minutes; drain, peel, and cube or slice. In the same pan the bacon was fried in, blend flour into reserved drippings. Cook over low heat 2 minutes, stirring constantly. Gradually stir in water, vinegar, sugar, and salt. Add onion and celery. Simmer over low heat 5 to 10 minutes or until celery is tender. Place sliced potatoes in a large bowl. Pour bacon mixture over potatoes; stir to coat potatoes. Serve hot.

Chef's Salad

Makes 8 servings

 1½ quarts mixed salad greens, coarsely torn
  1 cup sliced celery
  1 cup sliced cucumber
  ½ cup green pepper strips
  1 cup sliced carrots
  1 cup cauliflower, broken into flowerets
  2 large tomatoes, cut in wedges
  2 hard-cooked eggs, sliced
  1 cup Cheddar cheese strips
 1½ cups cooked ham strips
    Spicy French Dressing (recipe on page 47)

In a large salad bowl, combine salad greens, celery, cucumbers, green peppers, carrots, and cauliflower; toss lightly to mix. Arrange tomatoes, eggs, cheese, and ham attractively on top of salad greens. Serve with Spicy French Dressing.

Mustard and Pepper Relish

Makes about 6 pints

     5 sweet green peppers
     3 sweet red peppers
     3 large onions
     1 cup flour
     6 cups sugar
     3 cups vinegar
     1 cup water
     1 jar (7 ounces) prepared mustard
     2 tablespoons salt
     2 teaspoons turmeric
     2 teaspoons celery seed

Grind peppers and onions in a food grinder or chop in a food processor. In a large saucepan or Dutch oven, combine peppers, onions, and remaining ingredients; blend well. Cook over medium heat until thickened, stirring often. Pack boiling hot into clean hot jars to within ½ inch of the top. Seal with two-piece vacuum seal lids according to manufacturer's directions. Process in boiling water-bath canner for 10 minutes. Use on hot dogs, hamburgers, sandwiches, in ham salad, or as a dressing for potato salad.

Piccalilli

Makes about 7 pints

    20 green tomatoes
     1 medium head cabbage, cored
     6 large sweet green peppers
     6 large sweet red peppers
     6 medium onions
     1 cup salt
     3 quarts vinegar
     8 cups sugar
     2 tablespoons celery seed
     2 tablespoons dry mustard
     2 tablespoons whole cloves

Grind tomatoes, cabbage, peppers, and onions in food grinder or chop in a food processor. In a large bowl, combine vegetables and salt. Cover and let stand overnight. Drain; transfer vegetables to a large saucepan or Dutch oven. Add vinegar, sugar, and spices. Bring to boiling; boil 20 minutes, stirring often. Pack boiling hot into clean hot jars to within ½ inch of the top. Seal with two-piece vacuum seal lids according to manufacturer's directions. Process in boiling water-bath canner for 10 minutes.

Banana Pepper Relish

Makes about 6 pints

     8 cups banana peppers
     1 small head cabbage, cored
     1 tablespoon mustard seed
     3 tablespoons salt
     3 cups sugar
     3 cups vinegar

Grind peppers and cabbage in a food grinder or chop in a food processor. In a large bowl, combine peppers, cabbage, mustard seed, and salt. Let stand overnight. Drain; transfer vegetables to a large saucepan or Dutch oven. Add sugar and vinegar. Bring to boiling; boil for 20 minutes, stirring often. Pack boiling hot into clean hot jars to within ½ inch of the top. Seal with two-piece vacuum seal lids according to manufacturer's directions. Process in boiling water-bath canner for 10 minutes.

Green Tomato and Pepper Relish

Makes about 4 pints

     1 quart green tomatoes
     2 medium sweet red peppers
     2 medium sweet green peppers
     2 large onions
     1 small head cabbage, cored
     3 cups vinegar
     2 cups firmly packed brown sugar
     2 tablespoons mixed pickling spices

Grind tomatoes, peppers, onions, and cabbage in a food grinder or chop in a food processor. In a large bowl, combine all vegetables; let stand overnight. Drain well; squeeze out excess liquid. In a large saucepan or Dutch oven, combine vinegar and sugar. Place pickling spices in a spice bag or cheesecloth; tie securely. Add to vinegar mixture. Bring to boiling. Add vegetables; simmer about 30 minutes, stirring occasionally. Remove spice bag. Pack boiling hot into clean hot jars to within ½ inch of the top. Seal with two-piece vacuum seal lids according to manufacturer's directions. Process in boiling water-bath canner for 10 minutes.

Boiled Cole Slaw Dressing

Makes about 1½ cups

2 eggs
2 teaspoons flour
2 teaspoons dry mustard
1 cup sugar
1 cup cider vinegar

In a medium saucepan, combine eggs, flour, and mustard; blend well with a fork. Add sugar and vinegar. Bring to boiling over medium heat, stirring constantly. Remove from heat; let stand until room temperature. Store in a covered container in the refrigerator.

Tomato Soup Salad Dressing

Makes about 2 cups

1 can (10¾ ounces) condensed tomato soup, undiluted
¾ cup sugar
⅓ cup vinegar
1 cup vegetable oil
1 teaspoon celery salt
1 teaspoon garlic powder
1 teaspoon instant minced onion
1 teaspoon paprika
½ teaspoon black pepper
1 tablespoon Worcestershire sauce

In a medium bowl, combine soup, sugar, vinegar, and oil; blend well. Add all seasonings and Worcestershire sauce; blend well. Store in a covered container in the refrigerator.

Sour Cream Blue Cheese Dressing

Makes about 1½ cups

½ cup crumbled blue cheese
½ teaspoon salt
⅛ teaspoon black pepper
1 tablespoon minced onion
Dash Worcestershire sauce
1 teaspoon lemon juice
1 cup dairy sour cream

In a small bowl, combine blue cheese, salt, pepper, onion, Worcestershire sauce, and lemon juice; blend well. Stir in sour cream; blend well. Chill before serving.

Spicy French Dressing

Makes about 4 cups

1 can (10¾ ounces) tomato soup, undiluted
¾ cup vegetable oil
¾ cup sugar
½ cup vinegar
1 small onion, minced
1 teaspoon Worcestershire sauce
1 clove garlic, minced
1 teaspoon salt
¾ teaspoon black pepper
¾ teaspoon paprika
½ teaspoon dry mustard

In an electric blender or food processor, combine soup, oil, sugar, and vinegar; blend well. Add onion and seasonings; blend well. Store in a covered container in the refrigerator.

Cranberry Orange Fruit Dressing

Makes about 1⅔ cups

1 carton (8 ounces) vanilla-flavored yogurt
⅔ cup cranberry-orange sauce
½ teaspoon grated lemon peel
¼ teaspoon lemon juice

In a small bowl, combine yogurt, cranberry-orange sauce, lemon peel, and juice; blend well. Chill before using. Serve over fruit, such as apple wedges, melon balls, pineapple chunks, orange sections, banana slices, or grapes.

Sweet Sour Cream Dressing

Makes 1 cup

1 carton (8 ounces) dairy sour cream
3 tablespoons brown sugar or honey

In a small bowl, combine sour cream and brown sugar or honey; blend well. Serve with assorted fresh fruit.

Quick Russian Dressing

Makes about 1 cup

1 cup mayonnaise or salad dressing
4 tablespoons catsup
Dash Worcestershire sauce

In a small bowl, combine mayonnaise, catsup, and Worcestershire sauce; blend well. Chill before using.

Sauces and Marinades

Super Sauce

Makes about 1½ cups

- ¼ cup vinegar
- ½ cup water
- 2 tablespoons sugar
- 1 tablespoon mustard
- ½ teaspoon black pepper
- 1½ teaspoons salt
- ¼ teaspoon cayenne pepper
- 1 slice lemon
- 1 onion, sliced
- ¼ cup butter *or* margarine
- ½ cup catsup
- 2 tablespoons Worcestershire sauce
- 1½ teaspoons liquid smoke, optional

In a medium saucepan, combine vinegar, water, sugar, mustard, pepper, salt, cayenne, lemon, onion, and butter. Simmer, uncovered, 20 minutes, stirring occasionally. Add catsup, Worcestershire sauce, and liquid smoke, if desired; blend well. Bring to boiling. Remove from heat. Brush on ribs or chicken.

Cranberry Barbecue Sauce

Makes about 1¼ cups

- 1 can (8 ounces) jellied cranberry sauce
- ⅓ cup chili sauce
- 1 tablespoon Worcestershire sauce
- 1½ teaspoons lemon juice

In a small saucepan, place cranberry sauce; break up with a fork. Add remaining ingredients; blend well. Cook over medium-low heat until smooth. Brush on chicken or hamburgers. Pass remaining sauce at the table.

Jiffy Sauce

Makes about 1¼ cups

- 1 can (8 ounces) tomato sauce
- 2 tablespoons vegetable oil
- 1 tablespoon vinegar
- 1 tablespoon Worcestershire sauce
- 1 tablespoon instant minced onion
- 1 teaspoon salt
- ¼ teaspoon hot pepper sauce

In a small bowl, combine all ingredients; blend well. Brush on chicken, ribs, hot dogs, or hamburgers.

Beer-B-Q Sauce

Makes about 2½ cups

- ⅓ cup packed brown sugar
- 1 cup beer
- 1 cup catsup
- ⅓ cup vinegar
- 1 teaspoon dry mustard
- 1 teaspoon paprika
- ½ teaspoon chili powder
- ½ teaspoon salt
- 3 tablespoons Worcestershire sauce
- 1 medium onion, thinly sliced
- ½ lemon, thinly sliced
- 2 tablespoons cornstarch

In a medium saucepan, combine brown sugar, beer, catsup, vinegar, dry mustard, paprika, chili powder, salt, and Worcestershire sauce. Bring to boiling over medium heat, stirring frequently. Reduce heat and cook 5 minutes. Add onion and lemon. Simmer 5 minutes, stirring often. Remove about ¼ cup of sauce from pan. Stir cornstarch into reserved sauce until dissolved. Return to pan; blend well. Cook and stir 2 to 3 minutes or until thickened. Brush on chicken or ribs.

New Orleans Sauce

Makes about 1 cup

- 1 cup water
- 2 ounces bourbon
- 2 teaspoons soy sauce
- Dash Worcestershire sauce

In a small bowl, combine all ingredients. Brush on any kind of beef or game.

Orange and Raisin Sauce

Makes about 2 cups

- 1 can (6 ounces) frozen orange juice concentrate, undiluted
- 1½ cups water
- ½ cup sugar
- 1½ tablespoons cornstarch
- Salt
- ⅓ cup dark raisins

In a small saucepan, combine orange juice concentrate, water, and sugar. Add cornstarch; stir to dissolve. Cook over low heat until thickened, stirring frequently. Season with salt to taste. Stir in raisins. Brush on ham. Pass remaining sauce.

Lemon Barbecue Sauce for Chicken

Makes about 2 cups

- 1 cup butter *or* margarine
- 1 clove garlic, minced
- 4 teaspoons flour
- 2/3 cup hot water
- 1 tablespoon sugar
- 1 teaspoon black pepper
- 6 tablespoons lemon juice
- 1/4 teaspoon hot pepper sauce
- 1/2 teaspoon crushed leaf thyme
- 1 tablespoon salt

In a medium saucepan, melt butter. Add garlic; sauté until garlic is fragrant, 3 to 4 minutes. Stir in flour; cook 2 minutes, stirring constantly. Gradually stir in water until smooth. Add remaining ingredients. Cook until slightly thickened, stirring frequently. Let stand until cool. Dip chicken or shrimp in sauce before grilling.

Apricot Ginger Sauce

Makes about 1½ cups

- 1 jar (10 ounces) apricot preserves
- 3 tablespoons cider vinegar
- 2 tablespoons butter, melted
- 1/2 teaspoon ground ginger
- 1/2 teaspoon salt

In a small saucepan, combine all ingredients. Cook over low heat until preserves are melted and mixture is smooth, stirring constantly. Brush on chicken or pork the last 15 minutes of cooking time.

Country Terrace Barbecue Sauce

Makes about 2¾ cups

- 1/4 cup butter *or* margarine
- 3/4 cup sliced green onions
- 1/2 cup chopped celery
- 4 cups chopped peeled tomatoes *or* 2 cans (15 ounces each) tomato sauce with tomato bits
- 1/4 cup chopped parsley
- 1/4 cup packed brown sugar
- 1/4 cup vinegar
- 1½ teaspoons salt
- 2 tablespoons Worcestershire sauce

In a medium saucepan, melt butter. Add green onions and celery; sauté until vegetables are tender-crisp. Add tomatoes; simmer until vegetables are tender. Stir in remaining ingredients. Brush on chicken.

Deep South Hot Barbecue Sauce

Makes about 2¼ cups

- 2 tablespoons olive *or* vegetable oil
- 2 tablespoons instant minced onion, rehydrated
- 1/4 teaspoon instant minced garlic, rehydrated
- 2 tablespoons water
- 1 cup chicken broth
- 1 can (8 ounces) tomato sauce
- 1 can (6 ounces) tomato paste
- 3 tablespoons vinegar
- 2 tablespoons brown sugar
- 2 tablespoons parsley flakes
- 1/2 teaspoon ground allspice
- 1/4 teaspoon salt
- 1/4 teaspoon cayenne pepper

In a medium saucepan, heat oil. Add onion and garlic; sauté 4 minutes or until onion is golden. Remove from heat. Add remaining ingredients; blend well. Simmer, uncovered, 15 minutes, stirring occasionally. Brush on chicken, pork, or fish.

Smoky Barbecue Sauce

Makes about 2 cups

- 1 cup packed brown sugar
- 1 can (10¾ ounces) tomato soup, undiluted
- 1/4 cup butter *or* margarine
- 1/4 cup catsup
- 2 tablespoons prepared mustard
- 2 tablespoons liquid smoke
- 2 tablespoons lemon juice
- 1 tablespoon Worcestershire sauce
- 1 teaspoon onion powder
- 1/4 teaspoon garlic powder

In a medium saucepan, combine all ingredients; blend well. Bring to boiling over low heat, stirring frequently. Boil 1 minute; remove from heat. Brush on chicken, ribs, hot dogs, or hamburgers.

Western Sauce

Makes about 2¼ cups

- 1/2 cup packed brown sugar
- 3/4 cup catsup
- 1/2 cup cider vinegar
- 1/3 cup chili sauce
- 2 tablespoons prepared mustard
- 2 tablespoons steak sauce
- 1 tablespoon vegetable oil
- Dash hot pepper sauce
- 1 clove garlic, minced

In a small bowl, combine all ingredients; blend well. Brush on chicken, ribs, or hamburgers.

Marinades

Quick Steak Marinade

Makes about ½ cup

- ¼ cup steak sauce
- ¼ cup lemon juice
- 2 tablespoons vegetable oil
- 1 small onion, minced
- 1 clove garlic, crushed

In a small bowl, combine all ingredients; blend well. Place steak in shallow dish or in a double plastic bag. Pour marinade over steak. Cover or seal. Refrigerate 3 to 4 hours, turning steak once. Grill steak to desired doneness.

Lemon Marinade

Makes about 1½ cups

- ¾ cup vegetable oil
- 6 tablespoons soy sauce
- ¼ cup wine vinegar
- 3 tablespoons lemon juice
- 2 tablespoons Worcestershire sauce
- 1 tablespoon dry mustard
- 1 tablespoon salt
- 1½ teaspoons black pepper

In a small bowl, combine all ingredients; blend well. Place steak or roast in a shallow dish or in a double plastic bag. Pour marinade over meat. Cover or seal. Refrigerate 24 hours, turning meat occasionally. Grill meat to desired doneness.

Red Wine Marinade

Makes about 1½ cups

- ½ cup red wine
- ½ cup soy sauce
- ½ cup vegetable oil
- 2 tablespoons lemon juice
- 2 cloves garlic, minced
- 1 teaspoon salt
- ½ teaspoon ground ginger
- ½ teaspoon black pepper

In a small bowl, combine all ingredients; blend well. Place steak in a shallow dish or in a double plastic bag. Pour marinade over steak. Cover or seal. Refrigerate several hours or overnight, turning steak occasionally. Grill steak to desired doneness.

Pineapple Marinade

Makes about 2 cups

- ½ cup packed brown sugar
- 1 cup soy sauce
- ½ cup pineapple juice
- ½ cup vinegar
- 2 teaspoons salt
- ½ teaspoon garlic powder

In a medium saucepan, combine all ingredients; blend well. Bring to boiling; reduce heat and simmer 5 minutes. Refrigerate until chilled. Use to marinate shish kebabs or chicken.

Apple Tarragon Marinade

Makes about 2 cups

- 1 cup apple cider
- ⅓ cup vinegar
- ¼ cup vegetable oil
- 3 tablespoons honey
- 2 tablespoons steak sauce
- ⅓ cup sliced green onion with tops
- 1½ teaspoons crushed leaf tarragon
- 1 teaspoon salt
- ¼ teaspoon black pepper

In a medium saucepan, combine all ingredients. Bring to boiling; reduce heat and simmer, uncovered 20 minutes. Refrigerate until chilled. Use to marinate chicken or lamb.

White Wine Marinade

Makes about 1½ cups

- 1 cup white wine
- ½ cup vegetable oil
- ¼ cup minced celery
- ¼ cup minced onion
- 1 clove garlic, minced
- 1 teaspoon crushed leaf marjoram
- 1 teaspoon crushed leaf thyme
- ¼ teaspoon black pepper

In a small bowl, combine all ingredients; blend well. Place chicken or fish in a shallow dish or in a double plastic bag. Pour marinade over chicken or fish. Cover or seal. Refrigerate 3 to 4 hours. Grill as desired.

Marinades

Wild Game Marinade

Makes about 1 quart

- 2 cups dry red wine
- 1 cup wine vinegar
- 1 cup water
- 1 carrot, chopped
- 1 rib celery, chopped
- 1 large onion, chopped
- 2 cloves garlic, crushed
- 1 tablespoon mixed pickling spices
- ½ teaspoon black pepper

In a medium bowl, combine all ingredients; blend well. Place game, such as venison, in a large container. Pour marinade over meat. Cover and refrigerate 3 to 5 days for small cuts; 5 to 10 days for larger quantities. Makes enough marinade for up to 4 pounds of meat.

French Dressing Marinade

Makes about 1 cup

- 1 bottle (8 ounces) French dressing
- 1 cup dry red wine
- 1 clove garlic, minced
- 1 teaspoon chopped parsley
- ⅛ teaspoon crushed leaf tarragon
- ⅛ teaspoon crushed leaf thyme

In a small bowl, combine all ingredients; blend well. Place meat, fish, or vegetables in a shallow dish or in a double plastic bag. Cover or seal. Refrigerate 3 to 4 hours, turning once. Grill as desired. Use on chicken, lamb, fish, or vegetables.

Beef Marinade

Makes about 2 cups

- 1 cup tomato juice
- ½ cup vinegar
- 3 tablespoons chili powder
- 1 tablespoon brown sugar
- 1 tablespoon onion powder
- 1½ teaspoons salt
- ½ teaspoon crushed leaf oregano
- ½ teaspoon garlic powder

In a small bowl, combine all ingredients; blend well. Baste steaks, ribs, or hamburgers during grilling time.

Teriyaki Marinade

Makes about ¾ cup

- ¼ cup soy sauce
- ¼ cup red wine or 2 ounces bourbon or water
- 2 tablespoons sugar
- 1 teaspoon ground ginger
- 1 clove garlic, minced

In a small bowl, combine all ingredients; stir to dissolve sugar. Place steak in a shallow dish or in a double plastic bag. Pour marinade over steak. Cover or seal. Refrigerate 3 to 4 hours. Grill to desired doneness.

Dilled Wine Marinade

Makes about 3 cups

- 2 cups dry red or white wine
- ½ cup olive or vegetable oil
- 1 onion, thinly sliced
- 2 carrots, thinly sliced
- ¼ cup parsley sprigs or 4 teaspoons parsley flakes
- ¼ cup dill sprigs or 4 teaspoons dried dillweed
- ¼ cup minced chives
-   Dash pepper

In a medium bowl, combine all ingredients, blend well. Use to marinate fish or vegetables.

Hot Pepper and Herb Marinade

Makes about ¾ cup

- ¼ cup lime juice
- ½ cup vegetable oil
- ½ teaspoon sugar
- 1 teaspoon dry mustard
- 1 teaspoon salt
- ¼ teaspoon crushed leaf thyme
- ¼ teaspoon crushed leaf rosemary
- ¼ teaspoon crushed leaf basil
- 1 bay leaf
- ¼ teaspoon hot pepper sauce

In a small bowl, combine lime juice and oil; blend well. Add remaining ingredients; blend well. Place (beef or lamb) in a shallow pan or in a double plastic bag. Pour marinade over meat. Cover or seal. Refrigerate at least 5 hours, turning occasionally. Grill to desired doneness.

Condiments

Plantation Hot Sauce

Makes about 1½ cups

- ½ cup honey
- ½ cup prepared mustard
- ½ cup cider vinegar
- ¼ cup Worcestershire sauce
- 1 tablespoon chopped parsley
- 2 teaspoons hot pepper sauce
- 1 teaspoon salt

In a medium saucepan, combine honey and mustard; blend well. Stir in remaining ingredients. Bring to boiling over low heat, stirring often. Remove from heat. Serve warm with smoked fish or shrimp.

Cool Blender Sauce

Makes about 2¼ cups

- ¾ cup mayonnaise *or* salad dressing
- 1 egg
- 3 tablespoons lemon juice
- 1 teaspoon salt
- 1 teaspoon sugar
- 1 teaspoon instant minced onion
- 1 teaspoon prepared mustard
- 2 drops hot pepper sauce
- ⅛ teaspoon black pepper
- ¾ cup vegetable oil
- ⅓ cup chopped parsley
- 1 tablespoon prepared horseradish
- 1 clove garlic, minced

In an electric blender or food processor, combine first 9 ingredients; blend 3 to 4 seconds. With blender on, gradually add oil; blend until thick and smooth. Add parsley, horseradish, and garlic; blend until smooth. Serve with grilled or smoked fish.

Homemade Tomato Catsup

Makes about 10 pints

- 1 peck (12½ pounds) ripe tomatoes
- 8 medium onions, sliced
- ¼ teaspoon cayenne pepper
- 2 cups cider vinegar
- 1½ tablespoons broken stick cinnamon
- 1 tablespoon whole cloves
- 3 cloves garlic, minced
- 1 tablespoon paprika
- 1 cup sugar
- 2½ teaspoons salt

Wash and slice tomatoes. Boil tomatoes in a large kettle of water about 15 minutes or until soft. In a separate kettle, place onions. Add water just to cover; cook until tender; drain. Press tomatoes and onions through a sieve or process in an electric blender or food processor. Combine tomatoes and onion in a large saucepan or Dutch oven. Add cayenne; bring to boiling and boil rapidly until mixture is reduced to about half the original volume. While tomatoes are cooking, pour vinegar into a medium saucepan. Combine cinnamon, cloves, and garlic in a spice bag or piece of cheesecloth; tie securely. Add to vinegar. Bring to boiling; reduce heat and simmer 30 minutes. Bring to boiling; remove from heat; discard spice bag. Cover and set aside until ready to use. Add vinegar to tomato mixture. (There should be about 1¼ cups vinegar.) Add paprika, sugar, and salt; bring to boiling. Boil about 10 minutes until desired thickness, stirring often. Pour immediately into clean hot jars to within ½ inch of the top. Seal with two-piece vacuum seal lids according to manufacturer's directions. Process in a boiling water-bath canner for 10 minutes.

Lemon Catsup Sauce

Makes about 1 cup

- ¾ cup catsup
- 2 tablespoons steak sauce
- 1 tablespoon grated lemon peel
- 1 teaspoon lemon juice

In a small bowl, combine all ingredients. Serve over corned beef hash patties or hamburgers.

Tartar Sauce

Makes about ¾ cup

- ½ cup mayonnaise *or* salad dressing
- 1 tablespoon chopped ripe olives, optional
- 1 tablespoon chopped onion
- 1 tablespoon minced parsley
- 1 tablespoon sweet pickle relish

In a small bowl, combine all ingredients; blend well. Chill before serving with fish.

Appetizers

Oregano Dip

Makes about 1 cup

- 1 cup dairy sour cream
- 1 teaspoon crushed leaf oregano
- ½ teaspoon grated onion
- ¼ teaspoon salt
- Dash hot pepper sauce
- Assorted raw vegetables

In a small bowl, combine all ingredients, except vegetables; blend well. Chill at least 1 hour before serving.

Onion Smoked Fish Spread

Makes about 2 cups

- 2 cups flaked smoked fish
- ¾ cup mayonnaise or salad dressing
- ½ teaspoon onion powder
- 2 tablespoons chopped parsley
- Assorted chips, crackers, or raw vegetables

In a small bowl, combine all ingredients, except chips; blend well. Chill at least 1 hour before serving. Serve with chips, crackers, or raw vegetables.

Beach Balls

Makes 6 servings

- 1 can (7½ ounces) minced clams; drained; reserve liquid
- ½ cup butter or margarine
- ½ teaspoon poultry seasoning
- ¼ teaspoon salt
- 1 cup flour
- 4 eggs

Grease a large baking sheet; set aside. Preheat oven to 450° F. Add water to reserved clam liquid to equal 1 cup. In a saucepan, combine clam liquid, butter, poultry seasoning, and salt. Bring to boiling; reduce heat. Add flour; cook until mixture forms a ball, stirring constantly. Remove from heat. Add eggs, one at a time, beating well after each addition. Beat until shiny and smooth. Stir in clams. Drop dough by teaspoonfuls onto the prepared baking sheet. Bake 10 minutes; reduce heat to 350° F. and bake 10 minutes. Serve warm or cold.

Smoked Fish Spread

Makes about 3½ cups

- 1½ pounds smoked fish, skinned, boned, and flaked
- 1¼ cups mayonnaise or salad dressing
- 2 tablespoons minced sweet pickle
- 2 tablespoons chopped parsley
- 1 tablespoon mustard
- 2 teaspoons minced onion
- 2 teaspoons minced celery
- 1 clove garlic, minced
- ⅛ teaspoon Worcestershire sauce
- Assorted chips, crackers, or raw vegetables

In a medium bowl, combine all ingredients, except chips. blend well. Chill at least 1 hour before serving. Serve with chips, crackers or raw vegetables.

Fresh Fruit Dip

Makes about 4 cups

- 12 macaroon cookies, coarsely crushed
- ¼ cup firmly packed brown sugar
- 2 cups dairy sour cream
- 1 large pineapple
- Assorted berries
- Purple or red grapes, seeded, if necessary
- Seedless green grapes
- Sliced bananas
- Watermelon wedges
- Peaches, sliced
- Kirsch or brandy, optional

In a small bowl, combine macaroons, brown sugar, and sour cream; blend well. Chill several hours to soften macaroons. (Do not stir.) Cut a slice from pineapple about 1 inch below bottom leaves. Use a sharp knife to hollow out center, leaving shell intact. Cut pineapple pulp into bite-size pieces, discarding hard center core. Spoon sour cream dip into shell. Place pineapple in the center of a large serving platter. Arrange pineapple, berries, grapes, bananas, watermelon wedges, and peaches around pineapple. Sprinkle fruit with kirsch or brandy, if desired.

Appetizers

Pickled Shrimp

Makes 8 to 12 servings

- 2½ pounds fresh *or* thawed frozen shrimp
  Boiling water
- ½ cup celery tops
- ¼ cup mixed pickling spices
- 5 teaspoons salt, divided
- 2 cups sliced onions
- 7 bay leaves
- 1¼ cups vegetable oil
- ¾ cup vinegar
- 2½ tablespoons capers, undrained
- 2½ teaspoons celery seed
- 1½ teaspoons salt
  Dash hot pepper sauce

In a large saucepan, cover shrimp with boiling water. Add celery tops, pickling spices, and 3½ teaspoons of the salt. Simmer, covered, 5 minutes. Drain, cool, peel, shell, and devein shrimp. In a shallow dish, arrange shrimp and sliced onion. Add bay leaves. In a small bowl, combine oil, vinegar, capers and liquid, celery seed, remaining 1½ teaspoons salt, and hot pepper sauce; blend well. Pour marinade over shrimp and onions. Cover and refrigerate 24 hours. Drain marinade and serve.

Ham and Broccoli Cups

Makes 36

- 2 packages (10 ounces each) refrigerated butterflake rolls
- 1 tablespoon butter, softened
- 1 teaspoon lemon juice
- 2 tablespoons chopped onion
- 2 tablespoons chopped parsley
- 2 tablespoons prepared mustard
- ¾ cup shredded Cheddar cheese
- ¾ cup shredded mozzarella cheese
- 1 cup minced ham
- 1 cup minced broccoli, fresh *or* thawed frozen

Separate rolls; cut in halves. Press each half firmly into greased muffin cups. Bake in a 350° F. oven 5 minutes. If biscuits become too puffy, gently reshape. In a small bowl, combine butter, lemon juice, onion, parsley, and mustard; blend well. Add cheeses, ham, and broccoli; blend well. Spoon mixture by tablespoonfuls into partially baked cups. Bake 15 to 20 minutes or until hot and bubbly. These can be made ahead, frozen, thawed, and reheated on the grill.

Chili Dip

Makes about 1¼ cups

- 1 cup small curd cottage cheese
- 1 hard-cooked egg, finely chopped
- 1½ teaspoons grated onion
- 1 teaspoon chili powder
- ½ teaspoon salt
- 3 tablespoons pickle relish
- 1 tablespoon chopped stuffed olives
  Assorted chips, crackers, or raw vegetables

In a small bowl, combine cottage cheese, egg, onion, chili powder, and salt; beat with an electric mixer until smooth. Stir in pickle relish and olives. Cover and chill at least 1 hour before serving. Serve with chips, crackers, or raw vegetables.

Sausage Stuffed Mushrooms

Makes about 24 appetizers

- 1 pound fresh mushrooms
- 1 pound bulk pork sausage
- 1 clove garlic, minced
- 2 tablespoons chopped parsley
- 1½ cups shredded sharp Cheddar cheese
  Chopped, drained pimiento, optional
  Chopped parsley, optional

Rinse mushrooms; remove stems and pat dry. Chop stems. In a large skillet, combine chopped stems, sausage, garlic, and 2 tablespoons parsley. Cook until sausage is browned, stirring often; drain fat. Add cheese; stir until softened. Fill mushroom caps with sausage mixture. Place filled caps in a 13 x 9-inch baking dish. Bake at 350° F. 20 minutes or until cheese melts. Garnish with pimiento and parsley, if desired.

Taco Dip

Makes 8 servings

- 1 package (8 ounces) cream cheese, softened
- 1 can (10½ ounces) bean dip
- 1 package (1¼ ounces) taco seasoning mix, divided
- 2 cups shredded lettuce
- 2 large tomatoes, chopped
- 3 cups shredded Cheddar cheese
  Tortilla chips

In a bowl, combine cream cheese, bean dip, and half of the taco seasoning mix; blend well. Spoon into a shallow 8-inch serving dish. Top with lettuce, tomatoes, and Cheddar cheese. Sprinkle with remaining taco seasoning mix. Serve with tortilla chips.

Beverages

Golden Glow Punch

Makes 25 servings

- 1 can (6 ounces) frozen lemonade concentrate, thawed
- 1 can (6 ounces) frozen orange juice concentrate, thawed
- 1 can (6 ounces) frozen tangerine juice concentrate, thawed
- 2 cups water
- 2 bottles (28 ounces each) ginger ale, chilled
  Ice cubes

In a punch bowl or large pitcher, combine all juice concentrates and water; blend well. Just before serving, add ginger ale and ice cubes.

Spiced Iced Tea

Makes 12 to 16 servings

- 2 quarts water
- 12 tea bags
- 1 cup water
- ½ cup sugar
- ½ cup strained orange juice
- 1 cup strained lemon juice
- 12 whole cloves
- 2 cinnamon sticks

In a large saucepan, boil 2 quarts water. Add tea bags; let stand 5 minutes. Remove tea bags. In a small saucepan, combine 1 cup water and sugar; bring to boiling, stirring to dissolve sugar. Remove from heat. Add orange and lemon juices and spices to sugar water. Add spiced mixture to tea. Chill well before serving over ice in tall glasses.

Sea Foam Punch

Makes 12 to 16 servings

- 1 envelope (1½ ounces) unsweetened lemon-lime soft drink powder
- ½ cup sugar
- 1 quart cold milk
- 1 pint vanilla ice cream
- 2 bottles (7 ounces each) lemon-lime carbonated beverage, chilled

In a large bowl, combine soft drink powder, sugar, and milk; stir to dissolve soft drink powder and sugar. Add ice cream by spoonfuls. Carefully pour in lemon-lime carbonated beverage. Serve immediately.

Strawberry Rhubarb Punch

Makes 8 servings

- 3 cups sliced rhubarb
- 3 cups water
- 1 cup sliced strawberries
- 1 can (6 ounces) frozen pink lemonade concentrate, thawed
- ¾ cup sugar
- 1 cup ice cubes
- 2 bottles (7 ounces each) lemon-lime carbonated beverage
  Lemon slices, optional
  Strawberries, optional

In a large saucepan, combine rhubarb, water, strawberries, lemonade concentrate, and sugar; bring to boiling over high heat. Reduce heat and simmer, covered, 10 to 15 minutes or until rhubarb is very soft. Press through colander with back of spoon; discard pulp. Cover and refrigerate until cold. Pour strawberry-rhubarb syrup over ice cubes in a punch bowl. Add lemon-lime carbonated beverage. Garnish with lemon slices and strawberries, if desired.

Orange Blossom Punch

Makes 25 servings

- 1 cup cold water
- 1 jar (4 ounces) maraschino cherries, drained
- 1 can (8 ounces) pineapple chunks, drained
- 2 quarts orange juice
- 1 bottle (24 ounces) champagne

Fill a 6-cup ring mold with cold water. Drop in cherries and pineapple chunks. Place in freezer until frozen solid. At serving time, pour orange juice and champagne into a punch bowl. Unmold ice ring and slide into punch.

Cranberry Punch

Makes 12 to 16 servings

- 1 can (16 ounces) jellied cranberry sauce
- ¾ cup orange juice
- ¼ cup lemon juice
- 1 bottle (12 ounces) ginger ale, chilled
  Ice cubes

In a large pitcher, combine cranberry sauce and both juices. Chill. Just before serving, add ginger ale and ice cubes.

Desserts

Zucchini Banana Cake

Makes 12 to 16 servings

  3 cups flour
  2 teaspoons baking powder
  1 teaspoon baking soda
  1½ teaspoons cinnamon
  ½ teaspoon salt
  1 cup vegetable oil
  2 cups sugar
  4 eggs
  1½ cups grated zucchini
  1½ cups mashed bananas (about 3 medium)
  1 cup chopped nuts, optional

Grease and flour a 10-inch fluted tube pan. Preheat oven to 350° F. In a large bowl, combine flour, baking powder, baking soda, cinnamon, and salt; set aside. In a separate large bowl, combine oil and sugar; blend well. Add eggs; blend well. Blend in zucchini and bananas. Gradually blend in flour mixture. Stir in nuts, if desired. Pour into prepared pan. Bake for 1 hour 15 minutes or until a toothpick inserted in the center comes out clean. Cool in pan on a wire rack. Frost with a white or cream cheese frosting or glaze, if desired.

Summer Fruit Pie

Makes 4 to 6 servings

  ¾ cup graham cracker crumbs
  2 tablespoons butter or margarine, melted
  1 teaspoon sugar
    Dash cinnamon
  1 cup green or red grapes
  1 cup blueberries
  1 cup strawberry halves
  1 peach, peeled and sliced

In a small bowl, combine graham cracker crumbs, butter, sugar, and cinnamon; blend well. Press into a 9-inch quiche pan or pie plate. Bake at 350° F. 10 minutes or until lightly browned. Arrange fruit over crust. Brush on Currant Glaze. Store in the refrigerator.

Currant Glaze

  ¼ cup red currant jelly
  1 tablespoon water

In a small saucepan, combine jelly and water; cook over low heat 3 minutes or until jelly melts, stirring constantly.

Fresh Fruit Tart

Makes 12 servings

  1 package (9 ounces) lemon cake mix
  ⅔ cup graham cracker crumbs
  ½ cup chopped nuts
  ½ cup butter or margarine, softened
  1 egg
  1 package (3 ounces) cream cheese, softened
  ⅓ cup sugar
  ¼ teaspoon orange or vanilla extract
  1 cup whipping cream, whipped
  4 cups assorted sliced fresh fruit
  ⅓ cup apple jelly, melted

Preheat oven to 350° F. In a large mixing bowl, combine cake mix, graham cracker crumbs, nuts, and butter; blend at low speed until crumbly. Add egg; blend well. Press into a 14-inch pizza pan or 10 x 15-inch jelly-roll pan. Bake 10 to 15 minutes or until golden. Cool in pan on a wire rack. In a small bowl, combine cream cheese, sugar, and orange extract; beat until fluffy. Fold in whipped cream until well blended. Spread over crust. Arrange fruit decoratively on top. Brush with melted jelly. Store in the refrigerator.

Chocolate Cheese Dessert

Makes 12 servings

  ¾ cup shortbread cookie crumbs
  ⅓ cup ground nuts
  1 tablespoon sugar
  ¼ cup butter or margarine, melted
  1 carton (8 ounces) vanilla-flavored yogurt
  1 cup ricotta cheese
  1 can (16½ ounces) ready-to-spread milk-chocolate frosting
    Chopped nuts, optional

Preheat oven to 350° F. Grease a 9-inch springform pan; set aside. In a small bowl, combine cookie crumbs, nuts, sugar, and butter; blend until crumbly. Press mixture into bottom of prepared pan. Bake 8 minutes; let stand until cool. In a large bowl, combine yogurt, ricotta cheese, and frosting; beat on high speed 2 minutes or until smooth. Pour over cooled crust. Place in freezer 3 hours or until firm. Sprinkle nuts on top, if desired.

Desserts

Blueberry Parfait

Makes 8 servings

    1 package (3 ounces) lemon-flavored gelatin
    1 cup boiling water
    1 tablespoon grated lemon peel
    1 container (8 ounces) frozen whipped nondairy
        dessert topping, thawed
 1½ cups fresh blueberries

In a small bowl, dissolve gelatin in boiling water. Stir in lemon peel. Refrigerate until slightly thickened. Beat with an electric mixer until thick and fluffy. Fold in whipped topping until well blended. Spoon one-third of the gelatin into 8 tall dessert glasses. Top with about 1½ tablespoons blueberries. Repeat layers, ending with blueberries. Chill before serving.

Cherry Freeze

Makes about 10 servings

    1 package (3 ounces) cherry-flavored gelatin
    1 cup boiling water
    ½ cup sugar
    2 cups milk
    1 container (4 ounces) frozen whipped nondairy
        dessert topping, thawed

In a small bowl, dissolve gelatin in boiling water. Add sugar; stir until completely dissolved. Stir in milk. (Mixture will appear curdled, but will become smooth when frozen.) Pour into a 9 x 13-inch pan. Freeze about 1 hour or until ice crystals begin to form 1 inch from edge. Transfer to chilled bowl; beat with an electric mixer until smooth. Fold in whipped topping until well blended. Return to pan. Place in freezer about 4 hours or until firm. Scoop into individual serving dishes.

Bananas Foster

Makes 4 servings

    4 bananas
    ¼ cup butter or margarine
    ¼ cup packed brown sugar
    2 teaspoons rum extract
    ¼ teaspoon cinnamon
        Vanilla ice cream

Tear off 4 sheets of heavy-duty aluminum foil. Slice bananas lengthwise in half, then crosswise. Place bananas in center of foil. Dot each with butter. Sprinkle brown sugar, rum extract, and cinnamon over each. Wrap securely as shown on page 32. Grill over medium-hot coals 15 to 20 minutes or until bananas are tender. Remove bananas from foil; place in serving dishes. Top with scoops of vanilla ice cream.

Quick Orange Mousse

Makes 9 servings

 1¼ cups graham cracker crumbs
    ⅓ cup butter or margarine, melted
    ¼ cup sugar
    1 can (6 ounces) frozen orange juice concentrate,
        thawed
    1 jar (7 ounces) marshmallow creme topping
    1 cup whipping cream, whipped

In an 8-inch square baking pan, combine graham cracker crumbs, butter, and sugar; blend well. Press firmly onto bottom of pan. In a small bowl, combine orange juice concentrate and marshmallow creme; blend well. Fold whipped cream into marshmallow mixture. Pour into prepared pan. Place in freezer until frozen. Cut into squares.

Peaches 'n Cream Cheesecake

Makes 6 to 8 servings

    ¾ cup flour
    1 teaspoon baking powder
    ½ teaspoon salt
    1 package (3¼ ounces) vanilla-flavored pudding mix
    3 tablespoons butter or margarine, softened
    1 egg
    ½ cup milk
    1 can (16 ounces) sliced peaches, drained;
        reserve 3 tablespoons syrup
    1 package (8 ounces) cream cheese, softened
    ½ cup sugar
    1 tablespoon sugar
    ½ teaspoon cinnamon

Grease a 10-inch pie plate; set aside. In a large mixing bowl, combine flour, baking powder, salt, pudding mix, butter, egg, and milk; beat on low speed just until all ingredients are moistened. Beat on medium speed 2 minutes. Pour into prepared pie plate. Arrange peach slices on top of batter. In a small bowl, combine cream cheese, sugar, and reserved peach syrup; blend well. Spread cream cheese mixture over peaches. Preheat oven to 350° F. Combine sugar and cinnamon; sprinkle over cheesecake. Bake 30 to 35 minutes or until golden. Cool to room temperature. Serve warm or chilled. Store in the refrigerator.

Apple Upside-Down Cake

Makes 9 servings

    2 tablespoons butter *or* margarine
    ½ cup packed brown sugar
    1¼ cups sliced apples
        Pecan halves
    1 teaspoon cinnamon
    1 package (9 ounces) yellow cake mix

In a 9-inch baking pan, melt butter over low heat. Sprinkle brown sugar over bottom of pan. Arrange apple slices and pecans over brown sugar. Sprinkle cinnamon on top. Preheat oven to 350° F. Prepare cake mix according to package directions. Pour carefully over fruit. Bake 45 to 55 minutes or until top springs back when lightly touched. Cool in pan 5 minutes. Turn out of pan onto serving plate.

Peanut Butter Picnic Cake

Makes 12 to 16 servings

    2¼ cups flour
    2 cups packed brown sugar
    1 cup peanut butter
    ½ cup butter *or* margarine, softened
    1 teaspoon baking powder
    ½ teaspoon baking soda
    1 cup milk
    1 teaspoon vanilla
    3 eggs
    1 package (6 ounces) semisweet chocolate chips

Grease bottom only of a 9 x 13-inch baking pan; set aside. Preheat oven to 350° F. In a large mixing bowl, combine flour, brown sugar, peanut butter, and butter; beat until crumbly. Reserve 1 cup. Add baking powder, baking soda, milk, vanilla, and eggs; blend until smooth. Pour batter into prepared pan. Sprinkle reserved crumbs on top. Sprinkle chocolate chips over crumbs. Bake 35 to 40 minutes or until a toothpick inserted in the center comes out clean. Let stand in pan until cool. Cut into squares.

Lemon Fluff Pie

Makes 6 to 7 servings

    3 eggs, separated
    1 cup sugar, divided
        Grated peel and juice of 1 lemon
    3 tablespoons hot water
    1 baked 9-inch piecrust

In a mixing bowl, beat egg yolks until thick and light-colored. Gradually beat in ½ cup of the sugar, lemon peel and juice, and hot water. Pour into top of a double boiler. Cook until slightly thickened, stirring often. In a small mixing bowl, beat egg whites until foamy. Gradually beat in remaining ½ cup sugar; beat until stiff peaks form. Fold egg whites into custard. Spoon into piecrust. Chill until set.

Rhubarb Surprise Cake

Makes 12 to 16 servings

    3 cups cut-up fresh *or* thawed frozen rhubarb
    1½ cups water
    1 cup sugar
    1 package (3 ounces) strawberry-flavored gelatin
    2 cups miniature marshmallows
    1 package (18½ ounces) white cake mix
        Sweetened whipped cream, optional

In a large saucepan, combine rhubarb, water, and sugar. Bring to boiling; remove from heat. Add gelatin; stir to dissolve; set aside. Grease bottom only of a 9 x 13-inch baking pan. Sprinkle marshmallows over bottom of pan; set aside. Preheat oven to 350° F. Prepare cake mix according to package directions, using whole eggs. Pour batter over marshmallows. Pour rhubarb mixture evenly over batter. Bake 45 to 50 minutes or until lightly browned. Serve warm or cold topped with whipped cream, if desired.

Chocolate Chip Nut Squares

Makes 9 servings

    2 eggs, lightly beaten
    ¾ cup packed brown sugar
    ½ cup flour
    ½ teaspoon baking powder
    ¼ teaspoon salt
    ½ cup butter *or* margarine, melted
    1 cup semisweet chocolate chips
    ½ cup chopped walnuts, optional

Preheat oven to 325° F. In a mixing bowl, combine eggs and sugar; blend well. Add remaining ingredients; blend well. Spread batter in an 8 x 8-inch square baking pan. Bake 25 minutes or until sides begin to pull away from edge of pan. Cut into squares; let cool in pan.

Raspberry Dipped Fruits

Makes 10 to 12 servings

- ¼ cup shredded coconut
- 2 tablespoons finely chopped pecans
- 1 cup dairy sour cream
- ¼ cup raspberry preserves
- 2 tablespoons milk
  Assorted fresh fruit, such as apple and pear wedges, banana pieces, strawberries, grapes, and melon balls
  Lemon juice

In a small bowl, combine coconut, pecans, sour cream, preserves, and milk; blend well. If using apples, pears, or bananas, dip in lemon juice to prevent browning. Arrange fruit around edge of a large serving platter. Place dip on a bed of ice in center.

Strawberry Cheese Pie

Makes 8 to 10 servings

- ½ cup butter or margarine
- 1 cup flour
- 1 tablespoon sugar
- 1 egg yolk
  Pinch salt
- 1 package (8 ounces) cream cheese, softened
- ½ cup sugar
- 2 eggs
- 1 teaspoon vanilla
- 1 quart strawberries, hulled

In a small bowl, cut butter into flour and sugar with a pastry blender or two knives. Add egg yolk and salt; blend with a fork. Pat dough into a 9-inch pie plate. Bake at 375° F. 15 to 20 minutes or until golden. Let stand until cool. In a small bowl, combine cream cheese, sugar, eggs, and vanilla. Beat with an electric mixer until smooth. Pour into cooled piecrust. Bake at 375° F. 15 to 20 minutes or until set. Let stand until cool. Stand strawberries in pie shell. Spoon Glaze over berries. Refrigerate until well chilled.

Glaze

- 1 cup sugar
- 3 tablespoons cornstarch
- ¼ teaspoon salt
- ¾ cup fruit juice or water
- 1 teaspoon lemon juice

In the top of a double boiler, combine all ingredients; blend well. Simmer over slowly boiling water 20 minutes or until thickened, stirring frequently.

Banana Split Dessert

Makes 12 to 16 servings

- 2 cups graham cracker crumbs
- 5 to 6 bananas, sliced lengthwise
- ½ gallon French vanilla ice cream, slightly softened
- 1 cup chopped walnuts
- 1 package (6 ounces) semisweet chocolate chips
- ½ cup butter or margarine
- 2 cups powdered sugar
- 1½ cups evaporated milk
- 1 teaspoon vanilla
- 1 cup whipping cream, whipped

Butter a 9 x 13-inch pan. Reserve ½ cup of the graham cracker crumbs. Spread remaining crumbs in bottom of prepared pan. Arrange bananas on top of crumbs. Gently spread the ice cream on top of the bananas. Sprinkle nuts on top. Place in freezer until frozen. In a small saucepan, melt chocolate chips and butter over low heat, stirring constantly. Add powdered sugar and evaporated milk; blend well. Cook until thick and smooth, stirring often. Stir in vanilla. Pour sauce over ice cream. Return to freezer. Remove ice cream dessert from freezer 10 minutes before serving. Spread whipped cream over the top. Sprinkle on reserved graham cracker crumbs.

Fudge Brownies

Makes 18

- 1 package (12 ounces) semisweet chocolate chips
- 1 cup butter or margarine
- 4 eggs
  Pinch salt
- 1 cup sugar
- 1 cup sifted flour
- 1 teaspoon baking powder
- 2 teaspoons vanilla
- 1 cup chopped nuts, optional

Grease a 9 x 13-inch baking pan; set aside. Preheat oven to 375° F. Combine chocolate chips and butter in a large saucepan. Melt over low heat, stirring constantly. Remove from heat. In a small bowl, combine eggs, salt, and sugar; blend well. Add to chocolate mixture; blend well. Stir in flour, baking powder, and vanilla until well blended. Stir in nuts, if desired. Pour into prepared pan. Bake for 25 minutes or until brownie begins to pull away from edge of pan. Let stand until cool. Cut into bars.

Index